HEALING IS FOR YOU

By
Pastor Terry Mathews

Unless otherwise indicated, all Scripture quotations are taken from *The King James Version* of the Bible.

Direct quotations from the Bible appear in bold type.

Healing Is For You
ISBN 0-88144-211-9
Copyright © 2004 by
Terry Mathews
Published by Christian Publishing Services
PO Box 701434
Tulsa OK 74170

Printed in the United States of America. All rights reserved under International Copyright Law. Contents and/or cover may not be reproduced in whole or in part in any form without the express written consent of the author.

CONTENTS

LESSON 1: HEALING IS FOR YOU

Healing Is For You is a book designed to bring the Word of God to you and to anyone else that will listen to the truth that healing belongs to us.

God in His Word has provided healing and we are going to cover this subject thoroughly so you can be persuaded by the Word that healing belongs to you. We will deal with such things as:

1. Simple facts that healing is for you.
2. Healing comes through faith in God's Word.
3. Jesus was the Word made flesh and Jesus is the will of God in action.

God truly wants us well. As we begin to agree with that part of the gospel, just like we agree with the fact that God wants us saved from our sin, then God's Word goes to work in us to produce physical healing.

PSALM 107:19,20
19 Then they cry unto the LORD in their trouble, and he saveth them out of their distresses.
20 He sent his word, and healed them, and delivered them from their destructions.

How many of us know that sickness and disease can cause distress? He said they cried to the Lord and He saved them out of their distresses. Verse 20 simply says that God sent His Word to bring healing and deliverance to us from anything that would destroy.

PSALM 107:21
21 Oh that men would praise the LORD for his goodness, and for his wonderful works to the children of men!

Right away we begin to see that healing is a manifestation of God's goodness. Deliverance, then, is a manifestation of a wonderful work that God will do and truly has done in Christ. It is good to be well. You are at your best when you are well.

"He sent his word, and healed them..." (Psalm 107:20). God sent His Word and healed them in the old covenant, but thank God this old covenant scripture is for us today. If He did it for them in the old covenant, how much more would you think that God would do for us in the new? If He provided healing through His Word then, surely His Word today, because of Jesus, provides healing for us. Therefore, we can take great confidence in the fact that healing belongs to us and that healing is for you.

I began to look at the word "healed" and it ministered to me. In the Hebrew, it is the word ***rapha,*** which means "healed" or "healing". As you study out that meaning a little bit more, that word "healed" means "to cure." You could say, "He sent His Word to cure them." It also carries the meaning "to be a physician." Therefore, you could say, "He sent His Word to be a physician or to doctor them."

Now understand that anything that helps humanity is God's doing. In other words, we believe in doctors, hospitals and medicine. We believe in helping people wherever we can. So we are not here to put that down in any way. We are here to say that divine healing through the Word of God and through faith in that Word, belongs to every person on this planet who will dare believe it. And that includes you and your circumstance and your situation. You may have been bedfast for a long time, but the Word of God will work in you because He sent His Word and healed them.

One of the primary purposes that God sent His Word was to bring healing, to bring a cure, to doctor you. Another meaning of the word "healed" means "to make you whole." God sent His Word to make you whole. God's Word is still making people whole today. His Word will still doctor you today. His Word will still bring a cure to any sickness, infirmity, and disease that attaches itself to your body. Healing is for you and healing is for me. When you think about healing, you must understand that healing is primarily for the physical body. Now somebody says, "Well, you know their spirit needs to be healed." The Bible teaches in 1 Thessalonians 5, that man is a three part being. Man is a spirit, he has a soul, and he lives in a body. You are a spirit being. In other words, the real you is a spirit. You are made in God's image and God is a Spirit.

JOHN 4:24
24 **God is a Spirit: and they that worship him must worship him in spirit and in truth.**

MAN IS A SPIRIT

God is a Spirit. You are a spirit. I am a spirit. The spirit is the real me. I have a soul. My soul consists of my mind, my will, and my emotions. Personality is tied into that arena. We are really spirit, soul, and body. The body is not the most important part. The spirit is the most important part because the spirit is eternal and your body is temporary. When you die and leave this planet, your spirit will come out of that body and if you are born again, if you know Jesus as your Lord and Savior, you will depart and forever be with the Lord.

If you do not know Jesus as your Lord and Savior, then your spirit will depart and descend into hell to ever be separated from the presence of God. Somebody says, "Well, if God is love why does He send people to hell?" He doesn't. God has never sent anyone to hell. He has provided a way out. Because of man's sin and man's fall, man got on the road to destruction and Jesus became the exit. You get on that freeway and you see the exit sign.

The world is on a freeway called "the road to destruction" and Jesus has provided a way off. Jesus has provided a way out. He has provided a way for you to go to heaven. When you receive Him as your Lord and Savior, then you are on your way to heaven. Your spirit man is born again according to John 3. You are born again or "born of God."

That is a birth of the spirit. Well, then, if my spirit is born again, what about my soul? What do I do with my soul?

ROMANS 12:2
2 **And be not conformed to this world: but be ye transformed by the renewing of your mind, that ye may prove what is that good, and acceptable, and perfect, will of God.**

Romans 12:2 says we are to be transformed by the renewing of our minds. So our soul primarily is to be renewed through the Word of God. Why? So that we can think like God, act like God, and talk like God.

So many people don't think the thoughts of God. When I say that, I am talking about the thoughts that are in the Word. God said in Isaiah 55:8, that His thoughts are not man's thoughts and His ways are not man's ways. In other words, He said, "I think differently than man thinks." God has given us His Word so that we can agree with His thoughts. For instance, "He sent His Word and healed me." Do you agree with that thought? Have you renewed your mind to that thought of healing that comes from God? The mind has to be renewed to think like God. There are many different thoughts about healing today so I don't want to just give you my opinion. Let the Word begin to renew your mind so that you can think like God and truly receive healing for your physical body.

The point I want to make is simply this: For the most part, when we talk about healing it is not for the spirit. And for the most part, it is not for the mind, although, you can be sick in your soul and in need of transformation and healing that will come from the Word. But I am talking about physical healing. **I want to point out the fact that the word *rapha* applies to a cure for physical ailment: a physician for the physical body, making whole the physical man.**

HEALING IS PRIMARILY PHYSICAL

Jesus wants us well physically therefore, healing does belong to us. Many people at one time or another will argue the fact that physical healing belongs to us. However, no argument that stands against physical healing for your body is valid or scriptural. The Bible tells us over and over again that God Almighty, through the plan of redemption, has provided physical healing for us and healing is for you today. He sent His Word and healed them. Did you ever think about this? God in the Old Testament revealed Himself to His people through His covenant names. You may have heard some of the covenant names of God in the Old Testament. Jesus is God represented in the flesh to us, therefore, He is all those names.

GOD'S COVENANT NAMES

Let's review a few of God's covenant names: ***Jehovah Shalom,*** **the God of peace, or the God of prosperity, or the one that brings peace and prosperity to you.** God revealed himself to His people as ***Jehovah Shalom,*** the God of peace.

God also revealed Himself as ***Jehovah Nissi.*** That word, ***Nissi,*** means **the Lord my banner, or the Lord my Victory.** He is still the God of peace, is He not? He is still the God of victory. I do not think there is any Christian that is really born-again that would deny and denounce that.

How about another covenant name, ***Jehovah Shammah.*** The word ***Shammah*** means **the ever-present one.** He is still ever-present, isn't He?

MATTHEW 28:20
20 **Teaching them to observe all things whatsoever I have commanded you: and, lo, I am with you alway, even unto the end of the world. Amen.**

According to Matthew 28:20, we can see that Jesus is certainly the fulfillment of the covenant name, ***Jehovah Shammah.*** God is still ***Jehovah Shammah.*** He is all the while with us, ever-present God.

Another covenant name is ***Jehovah Rohe,*** **the God who is my shepherd.** Oh, how often we quote the 23rd Psalm. *"The Lord is my shepherd; I shall not want"* (Psalm 23:1). I've heard it at almost every funeral I have been to. Most of the time, people use the 23rd Psalm as a scripture reading, and that's wonderful. Anytime you use the Word it is powerful, but Psalm 23 is a psalm for living—not just one for dying.

JOHN 10:11
11 **I am the good shepherd: the good shepherd giveth his life for the sheep.**

That's ***Jehovah Rohe.*** He is still our Shepherd. Nobody would deny that.

And then there is ***Jehovah Jireh,*** **my provider.** I like the literal translation of that which is: **the one who goes into the future to make sure there is provision before I get there.** We sing it, we believe it, and we call upon His name and ask Him for His provision. Look at Philippians 4:19.

PHILIPPIANS 4:19
19 But my God shall supply all your need according to his riches in glory by Christ Jesus.

He is still ***Jehovah Jireh.*** He is still our Provider.

Another covenant name is ***Jehovah Tsidkenu.*** It means, **the Lord my righteousness.** He is the one that grants us right standing or righteousness through our faith in Jesus. We can see in the New Testament that He is still our righteousness.

2 CORINTHIANS 5:21
21 For he hath made him to be sin for us, who knew no sin; that we might be made the righteousness of God in him.

Now if we can look at all these covenant names and know that God is still our peace, our victory, our ever-present God, our shepherd, and our provider, then why would we do away with ***Jehovah Rapha,*** which means, **I am the Lord that healeth thee?** Why would we take that one out of its setting and say, "Well, I guess Jehovah Rapha is not interested in healing my physical body anymore?" If you accept the other covenant names, then you have to accept this one.

He is still the God that healeth thee, and healing still belongs to you and me today. There is no way around it from scripture. It is ours. We have it by faith in Jesus. We can claim it through the power of His Word. He sent His Word and healed them. ***Jehovah Rapha*** is still the God that heals us. Let's look at the following scriptures.

MALACHI 3:6
6 For I am the LORD, I change not…

HEBREWS 13:8

8 Jesus Christ the same yesterday, and to day, and for ever.

If God healed in the Old Testament, if He was ***Jehovah Rapha*** then, He is still ***Jehovah Rapha*** now. He is still our healer. He is still our provider. He is still the God of peace. Believe His promise, believe His Word. You shall be established in healing.

Let me show you another scripture in the New Testament:

HEBREWS 8:6

6 But now hath he obtained a more excellent ministry, by how much also he is the mediator of a better covenant, which was established upon better promises.

Now is the day for your healing. Now is the moment for your faith to rise up and believe that healing belongs to you. Hebrews 8:6 is talking about Jesus. We just read in the Old Testament *"I am the Lord that healeth thee..."* (Exodus 15:26). Then we get over here in the New Testament and it says that Jesus, who is Jehovah, has come and obtained a more excellent ministry. He is the high priest of this new covenant. In other words, He will see to it that His Word comes to pass in our lives if we believe it. He has got a more excellent ministry and *"...He is the mediator of a better covenant, which was established upon better promises."* (Hebrews 8:6)

We don't have it worse than they had it in the Old Testament—we have it better! We don't even have the same covenant. We have a better covenant! **If God healed then, He is healing today. Healing is for you and healing is for me.** Thank God for His promise and thank God that healing belongs to you.

Remember this fact: **We have a better covenant, and it is built on better promises. It is absolutely signed and sealed in the blood of Jesus. In that covenant there is healing for your physical body.**

NOTES

LESSON 2: JEHOVAH RAPHA

Physical healing belongs to you today through the death, burial, and resurrection of Jesus. After all, Jesus did not come just to do something for one part of your being.

> 1 THESSALONIANS 5:19
> **And the very God of peace sanctify you wholly; and I pray God your whole spirit and soul and body be preserved blameless unto the coming of our Lord Jesus Christ.**

Man is a spirit; he has a soul, and lives in a body. So if Jesus just came to give you a new birth or a new spirit and not do anything about your soul, which consists of your mind, will and emotions, and not do anything about your physical body, then it would only be a partial redemption.

The Bible said in the book of Hebrews that we have a complete redemption—not a partial redemption, and an everlasting release. So healing is for you today. I want to share with you this rich promise of the Word of God so that you can rise up in faith and receive and maintain your physical healing.

Did you know that approximately one third of our national budget is spent on healthcare in the form of Medicare and Medicaid? That translates into about two hundred and fifty billion dollars. What do you think that figure is when we talk about individual care, such as our HMO's, our prescriptions, and doctor care? It translates into literally hundreds of thousands and millions of dollars. Therefore, healing is a real need.

You have a physical body. It is attacked with symptoms or disease. Sickness is a thief. It robs you of your health, your well being, your family, your finances, your joy and your peace—all the things that Jesus came to give. Jesus brought the opposite of sickness—He brought healing. Actually, He brought health. He brought the joy, the peace, and the restoration.

When you think about healing, it is really number two on God's priority list as recorded in 3 John 2.

3 JOHN 2
2 Beloved, I wish above all things that thou mayest prosper and be in health, even as thy soul prospereth.

So God's greatest desire is your financial well being and your physical well being. You need both of these to be effective for God, for your family, and for yourself in the earth.

Let's look at Exodus 15:26. This scripture just nails this healing issue down because we know that God is the same yesterday, today and forever. He changes not.

EXODUS 15:26
26 And said, If thou wilt diligently hearken to the voice of the LORD thy God, and wilt do that which is right in his sight, and wilt give ear to his commandments, and keep all his statutes, I will put none of these diseases upon thee, which I have brought upon the Egyptians: for I am the LORD that healeth thee.

Now God made this statement to the children of Israel after they had come out of Egypt land. They had crossed the Red Sea (in chapter 14) and God brought them to that point of unique glorious deliverance. They came to the Red Sea in front of them, the mountains and the desert on each side, and then Pharaoh's army was coming in hot pursuit behind them. God said to Moses, "Stretch forth your rod."

We have a rod today and it is a rod of authority. It is the name of Jesus. If you are born again, you've got the name of Jesus. It belongs to you and you can stretch forth that rod against the devil and the cohorts of hell and command them to get out of your way.

Moses stretched forth the rod and you know what happened. The sea parted and the children went through on dry ground. Then, when Pharaoh and his hosts tried to do the same, God closed the Red Sea and they drowned. Really, God said to them, "This enemy that you see today, you will see no more forever." Too many times we deal with the same problems over and over and over—the same sicknesses, the same diseases, the same temptations, and the same sins—when God is saying, "I have provided a way for you to have absolute victory over that situation and be free from that problem."

In this case, we're talking about being free from that sickness because healing is for you. Actually, healing is good, but divine health is better. **God's ultimate goal is for us to receive our healing and enter on into divine health, and walk with peace of mind, peace in our spirit, and peace in our body.**

THE WATERS OF MARAH MADE SWEET

God brought the children of Israel out and they began to sing and rejoice in song, *"...I will sing unto the LORD, for he hath triumphed gloriously: the horse and his rider hath he thrown into the sea."* (Exodus 15:1) They were having a shouting time. Then they moved on a little bit and went through the wilderness and they couldn't find any water. So they started complaining. When they found water, it was the waters of Marah.

EXODUS 15:23-25

20 And when they came to Marah, they could not drink of the waters of Marah, for they were bitter: therefore the name of it was called Marah.

21 And the people murmured against Moses, saying, What shall we drink?

22 And he cried unto the LORD; and the LORD showed him a tree, which when he had cast into the waters, the waters were made sweet: there he made for them a statute and an ordinance, and there he proved them,

Moses took that tree and threw it into the waters and the waters were made sweet. This tree represents the cross of Calvary. It is a type and shadow of the tree that Jesus, our Lord, gave His life upon so that the bitter waters of our life could be made sweet. I don't know about you, but when I came to Jesus, He transformed me and made my life sweet. I was changed by His power.

Notice what He said, *"...there he made a statute and an ordinance..."* (vs. 25). Did you ever notice that before? God said, "I am going to set a decree in motion." This decree is unchangeable. We can follow it right on through the Old Testament into the New Testament and see that it was an ordinance that God established for His people. What was the ordinance? Notice what it was.

EXODUS 15:26

26 And said, If thou wilt diligently hearken to the voice of the LORD thy God, and wilt do that which is right in his sight, and wilt give ear to his commandments, and keep all his statutes, I will put none of these diseases upon thee, which I have brought upon the Egyptians: for I am the LORD that healeth thee.

Right there, God said that He doesn't put disease upon you. Some folks think, "God gave me this sickness to teach me a lesson." No, He didn't. God doesn't teach lessons with sickness. He teaches us by His Word and by His Spirit. Now you may have gotten sick because of disobedience. You may have gotten yourself into a position where the devil came in and put something on you. I don't know anything about your situation, and I'm not saying every case is that way. What I am saying is that God did not put sickness on you. Don't blame Him for that.

How would you like your children to blame you for something evil that is destroying their life and robbing them of their health and well-being? God did not put sickness on you. If you believe God put it on you then how are you going to believe that He wants you well? It would be hard to release your faith in the fact that Jesus took sickness for you. If God put it on you and Jesus took it for you, then Jesus is doing something against God. They would be opposing each other and that is not the case.

So God said that's an ordinance, that's a statute. "I will not allow or put any disease upon you that came upon the Egyptians." God did not put sickness on you. Settle that in your mind. If you are going to receive healing, you have got to settle that fact. **It is not God's will for you to be sick. It is God's will for you to be well.** How do we know that? Because Jesus is God's will. Jesus took our infirmities and bore our sicknesses and disease. That ought to be good news for you today. Say, "Thank God, He does want me well! If He wants me well, bless God, I can be well! I will rise up out of this sick bed and receive my healing in Jesus' name."

Now lets look at another thing here. God said, "I will not allow (that's causative verb) any of these diseases to be upon you." King James says, "I will not put them on you." God is not allowing it. God is not putting in on you. God is not causing it. Many times we get ourselves in a position where the devil has access through a lack of knowledge, ignorance, disobedience, or sin to come in and cause the problem. Whatever the case may be, the bottom line is this: **God wants you well.** For He said, *"I am the Lord that healeth thee,"* (Exodus 15:26).

Now did you know this scripture here in verse 26 of Exodus 15 is the scripture that translates, I am ***Jehovah Rapha?*** The covenant names of God have not changed. If He ever was ***Jehovah Rapha,*** then He is still ***Jehovah Rapha*** now. I would circle or underline this scripture where God said, **"I am."** He didn't say, "I was" or "I will be" or "I'll be for a time." When God says, "I am" something, He means, "He am" something. And if "He am" something, then "He am" something now. He said, "I am" to them—"I am the Lord that healeth thee!" God wants us well. Healing is for us.

It has blessed me so much just to take a literal translation of this scripture. It literally translates this way: **"I exist eternally to thoroughly make you whole."** God says that one reason He exists is for your well being—your physical healing. One reason He sent His Son was to make you whole.

Now, we believe Jesus died for our sins. We receive it by faith and declare that we are righteous and on our way to heaven through Christ. **The same Jesus that took our sins took our sickness physically upon His body.** With His stripes you were healed. God said My very existence is proof that I want you well. I am going to receive my healing. I am going to believe it. I am going to act on it, build my faith in it because the Bible teaches us that healing is for us today.

JESUS IS THE HEALING WORD

Boldly say in your heart and in your mind, to your friends, to your family, to yourself, to the devil, and to the Lord, *"I believe healing is for me!"* That is the starting point for you to receive your miracle.

Remember in Psalm 107:20 it says, *"He sent his word, and healed them..."* John 1:1 tells us that Jesus is the Word of God. So, if Jesus is the Word of God, and God sent His Word to heal them, then obviously He sent Jesus to bring physical healing to people. The word "healed" there in Psalm 107:20 means "to cure." God sent Jesus to bring a cure for you. It also means, "to be a physician" or "to doctor." The Word will doctor you and make you whole.

JOHN 1:1-4
1 In the beginning was the Word, and the Word was with God, and the Word was God.
2 The same was in the beginning with God.
3 All things were made by him; and without him was not any thing made that was made.
4 In him was life; and the life was the light of men.

This passage of scripture is a very important key to healing. The Word was involved in creating all things. In the Word was life and the life was the light of men. Now verse 4 says *"In him..."* referring to the Lord.

Notice verse 11 of John 1:

JOHN 1:11
11 He came unto his own, and his own received him not.

Have you received Jesus today as your Lord and Savior? Have you opened your heart and received the gift that God has given? This is a book about healing for your physical body, but what is more important than salvation? If I had a choice, I would rather be saved in my spirit and sick in my body and still go to heaven, than to be full of sin in my spirit and have a well body and go to hell. But the wonderful thing is that the plan of redemption provided both salvation for your spirit and healing for your body. We have a complete redemption.

You can receive Jesus as your Lord and Savior by just simply saying, "Lord, come into my life. Forgive my sin. I believe you are alive. I believe you rose from the dead and I confess you as my Lord." Jesus will come into you heart.

He said in verse 12,

JOHN 1:12
12 But as many as received him, to them gave he power to become the sons of God, even to them that believe on his name:

Do you believe on His name? If you do, you are a member of God's family. You have become a son or daughter of God. Your spirit is born again. Now you can receive physical healing for your body because He purchased it at the same time.

Now verse 14,

JOHN 1:14
14 And the Word was made flesh, and dwelt among us, (and we beheld his glory, the glory as of the only begotten of the Father,) full of grace and truth.

This scripture is talking about Jesus. How do we know? Because verse 17 goes on to tell us,

JOHN 1:17
17 For the law was given by Moses, but grace and truth came by Jesus Christ.

Psalm 107:20 said *"He sent his word, and healed them..."* Exodus 15 says I am ***Jehovah Rapha.*** And we find in John 1:14 that Jesus is the Word. **Jesus is Rapha. Jesus is the doctor that God sent to make you well and if God sent Him to make you well then healing belongs to you in His mighty name!** And you can start claiming that deliverance and that healing by faith in Jesus Christ today.

Simply start by saying, "I believe that God wants me well. In the name of Jesus, I resist sickness and disease. By faith, I receive my healing."

You watch what God will do. He will start working in your life bringing to pass His perfect will, which is healing for your body.

Jesus is the living Word of God and God sent Him to make us well. He is ***Jehovah Rapha,*** the Lord that heals us.

LESSON 3: GOD'S WORD IS MEDICINE

HEALING BELONGS TO YOU

Healing belongs to you. If you are sick in bed, at home, in a nursing home, hospital, or wherever, you can begin to understand and rest assured in your heart that healing is part of our redemption. You remember one of the theme text scriptures is Psalm 107:20.

PSALM 107:20
20 He sent his word, and healed them, and delivered them from their destructions.

God said He sent His Word to bring healing. That word "healed" there is the word ***rapha.*** It means "to cure, to doctor, or to be a physician." It means "to make whole." We understand ***Jehovah Rapha*** is still available to us today. That is one of the covenant names of God. It means, "I am the Lord that healeth thee, or I exist eternally to thoroughly make you whole." God is saying that part of His existence is to see to it that His Word concerning healing comes to pass in your life.

GOD SENT HIS WORD AND HEALED THEM

God sent His Word and healed them. Verse 14 of John 1 says,

JOHN 1:14
14 And the Word was made flesh, and dwelt among us, (and we beheld his glory, the glory as of the only begotten of the Father,) full of grace and truth.

We beheld His glory. John's writing said we recognize now that this man called Jesus was the Word of God in person. We walked with Him, we talked with Him, and we beheld His glory. **The Word is a person and His name is Jesus.** Psalm 107 said He sent His Word and healed them. Well, if He sent His Word in the old covenant to bring healing, then He sent His Word, Jesus in the new covenant to bring healing. Part of God's plan of redemption includes healing for your physical body.

DIVINE HEALTH

God wants you well and God wants me well. He doesn't want us to have to spend our income and our life trying to stay well through natural means. He wants us to walk by supernatural strength, power and faith and receive our healing. He wants us to live in divine health. We are not opposed to doctors, you understand. Doctors can help people. I've been to doctors myself, and my children have been to doctors. We don't oppose anything that helps people. But don't stop there. Don't camp out and be satisfied with just that. Go on to God's great redemptive plan because Jesus Christ is the Word of God, and God sent Him to heal us.

One reason that Jesus came was to bring us physical healing. There is just no way to get around that. It is provided for us. You say, "Well, how come so many people are sick?" Many times that happens because people do not know that healing has been provided for them. They have never been taught. In some cases, they've been taught the very opposite—that God used to heal in the Bible days, but that He doesn't heal any more because now we have doctors, and so on and so forth. Well, thank God again for doctors. **But they are not God's solution to disease. Jesus is.**

Look at verses 15 through 17 of John 1:

JOHN 1:15-16
15 John bare witness of him, and cried, saying, This was he of whom I spake, He that cometh after me is preferred before me: for he was before me.
16 And of his fulness have all we received, and grace for grace.
17 For the law was given by Moses, but grace and truth came by Jesus Christ.

"...of his fulness have we received..." (verse 16). Think about this. How healthy do you think Jesus is? How much life is in Him? All life is in Him. Because the Bible said in verse 4, *"...in him was life..."* As a matter of fact, one of His names in the Bible is called the Life.

JOHN 14:6
6 Jesus saith unto him, I am the way, the truth, and the life:

JESUS IS TOTAL HEALTH

So, how healthy is Jesus? He is total health. He is total life. He said you and I receive some of that fullness. God is not passing out sickness today. He is not passing out infirmity or weakness or disease. God does not make His children sick. He sent His Son, according to John 10:10, that we might have life and have it more abundantly. He wants us to have forgiveness of sin, newness of life, and physical healing. It is all through the Bible that Jesus took our infirmities and bore our sicknesses and our disease, and by His stripes we are healed. Now the point I want to bring out is this: **We have got some of His fullness available to us today.**

There is enough life in Jesus to go around. And there is enough life in Him to make you well. I'm telling you now, just a little bit of the life of God flowing into you will wipe out cancer, disease, and all types of infirmity and make you every whit whole. It is the very essence of who God is and what He has provided. That is some of what we receive when we accept the promises of God concerning physical healing by faith.

GOD NEVER CHANGES

Don't talk yourself out of it. Because God is the same yesterday, today, and forever. He changes not.

HEBREWS 13:8
8 Jesus Christ the same yesterday, and to day, and for ever.

If He ever was ***Jehovah Rapha,*** the Lord that healeth thee, then He is still ***Jehovah Rapha*** today. And if He ever sent His Word to heal, then He is still sending His Word forth.

Faith is something that has to develop and has to grow and that is why some people never walk in healing because they never take the time to find out what God's Word says about it.

Look at Proverbs, chapter 4.

PROVERBS 4:20-23
20 My son, attend to my words; incline thine ear unto my sayings.
21 Let them not depart from thine eyes; keep them in the midst of thine heart.
22 For they are life unto those that find them, and health to all their flesh.
23 Keep thy heart with all diligence; for out of it are the issues of life.

Now when He uses the word "heart," He is talking about the center of your being, or your spirit man. Remember you are a three-part being. You are a spirit, you have a soul, and you live in a body. God is saying, "Take my words and incline your ear to them, give attention to them. Keep them in front of your eyes so that they will stay in the midst of your heart."

GOD'S WORD IS FAITH FOOD

God's Word is spirit food. God's Word is faith food. When you feed upon God's Word, it builds up your spirit man. Jesus is the living Word of God. The Bible is the written Word of God. If we will feed upon the written Word, then we will get to know the living Word. And if we get to know the living Word, healing can be a result of knowing Him. Healing comes as a result of knowing the Word.

Notice verse 22, *"For they are life unto those that find them, and health to all their flesh."* God's Words are life to those that find them and health to all their flesh. Jesus provided healing for us, but the written Word is the connection to the living Word.

If Jesus Himself can bring healing to your body, then the written Word of God can bring healing to your body. "Whose report will you believe?" one songwriter said. "We shall believe the report of the Lord." You get a doctor's report; you get this report and that report. You have a report from God in the Word. You can look at your physical body and you can see in the natural that you need healing manifested in your body. But if you just look at that all the time and that's all you ever see, then you'll never see the promise of God.

LOOK AT THE WORD

Go look at the Word. Go look at the promises of God. Get a hold of some tapes and videos that will help you get the Word of God in your spirit. Why? Because His Words are life **to those that find them.** There's got to be some study, some looking, and some effort involved in finding something. As you give attention to the Word, you are going to receive life. Then He said that life would be the same life that is in Him. It is part of that fullness that we receive from Him.

When that life is imparted into you because you have meditated on the Word and you have faith in Jesus and in His name, it will bring healing. It will bring health, and it will bring strength. Notice the last part of verse 22, "[My Words are] *health to all their flesh."* The margin says *"medicine* to all their flesh." **God's Word is medicine.** If you had cancer, and I told you today that there is a new prescription drug on the market, and they were having tremendous results in fighting cancer and in ridding cancer cells from people, you would see to it that you got your hands on it. You would take it faithfully. But I want you to know the miracle manna from heaven is here. It is the Word of God and the Bible says it is medicine to all our flesh.

If you will take this Word faithfully and believe God's promises, if you will put it in your mouth and get it in you heart, then you can have healing now! Healing is for you and God has given you a whole book of medicine. Begin today to take God's medicine by reading His promises, putting them in your mouth and saying, "Healing belongs to me now!" He sent His Word and healed you. God's Word is medicine to all our flesh. Medicine won't do you any good just sitting on the shelf and neither will God's Word. As you get God's promises concerning healing into your heart by meditating on them, thinking about them and speaking them, they will produce healing in your body.

Get the Word and just concentrate on it. Hear the Word, see the Word, and let God fill you with His life and His healing power.

Great things are a result of standing upon the promises of God. Remember this, **God sent His Word and healed you, therefore, healing is yours today by faith in Jesus.**

LESSON 4:
ATTEND TO GOD'S WORD

Sickness is not your friend. It is an enemy and it comes to steal, kill and destroy you. It comes to rob you of your health, your well being, your finances, your family, your peace, and your joy. Jesus came that we might have life and have it more abundantly.

PUT GOD'S WORD FIRST

Proverbs 4:20 says,

PROVERBS 4:20
20 My son, attend to my words; incline thine ear unto my sayings.

If God says for us to do something, obviously we have the ability to do it. And, it is our responsibility to do it if we are going to receive the benefits of it. He said *"...attend to my words..."* That word "attend" means "give attention to" God's Word. Put God's Word first place. So many people put all kinds of things first place. If we are not careful, we will put the doctor's report first place.

ISAIAH 53:1
1 Who hath believed our report? and to whom is the arm of the LORD revealed?

It is obvious to me the arm of the Lord, or the strength of the Lord, is revealed to the one who believes His report. God is looking for somebody to believe. God is looking for somebody that will stand upon the covenant. Stand upon the promise and believe God's Word. Put His Word first place because His Word is His report. So you just can't believe the doctor's report first. You have got to believe God's report first. Sometimes, the doctor's report doesn't agree with God's report. When that happens, you've got to make a choice as to which report you will believe. Believe the report of the Lord! Give God's report, or Word, first place.

Do you know a lot of people believe their church doctrine report over the Bible? I'm not against churches. I pastor a good church. I believe in churches. I believe in people being a part of a church. But you should not believe your church creed over the Bible. Because you church creed may be wrong. We have to stay open to revelation and instruction from the Lord. I believe in all good churches that are preaching the gospel. However, many people never receive their healing because their churches don't believe in it. You can't even believe the report of your pastor over God's report. If your pastor is not preaching the Word, then find out what the Word says and believe that. Find out what God's Word says about healing.

Did you know that you can go to a good church and get saved and go to heaven and be as sick as a dog? Because faith has to be exercised in every part of God's promises. Just because you are sick doesn't mean that you are a sinner. There's an open door somewhere and the devil has taken advantage of you and brought that disease on you. God did not put it on you. Many times it is simply because we don't know what God says.

God said, "Incline your ear to my saying." **Listen to the Word. Hear the Word.** You are getting enough negative report. It is all around you. It is on every television program. It is time you hear God's report. Keep it in front of your eyes. Don't let it depart from your heart. Keep God's Word in your spirit. Keep your spirit man full of the Word.

LUKE 5:15
15 But so much the more went there a fame abroad of him: and great multitudes came together to hear, and to be healed by him of their infirmities.

Hear and be healed. The multitudes came to hear Jesus and to be healed. So as you hear the Word of God, healing will come.

Now, back to Proverbs chapter 4:

PROVERBS 4:22
22 For they are life unto those that find them, and health to all their flesh.

So God said if you attend to His report, if you find His promises concerning healing, they will produce life in you. Say, "God's

Word produces life in me!" That's a good confession to make. "God's Word produces life in me! God's Word is medicine to all my flesh!" We have some miracle medicine today given to us by God in the Word. God sent His Word to heal us. So as you study these lessons on healing, it is like taking medicine and it is producing life in you.

DESTROYED FOR LACK OF KNOWLEDGE

Notice Hosea 4:6.

HOSEA 4:6
6 My people are destroyed for lack of knowledge:

God says My people are destroyed for a lack of knowledge. And so then, knowledge about God's plan of redemption becomes very, very important to us. If we are not going to be destroyed, or cut off, or perish, we have got to know what God says about the subject.

It is vitally important that we find out what God says concerning healing if we are going to believe it and have medicine for our flesh. It will keep us from being destroyed. It will cause us to be healed.

ISAIAH 53:1-5
1 Who hath believed our report? and to whom is the arm of the LORD revealed?
2 For he shall grow up before him as a tender plant, and as a root out of a dry ground: he hath no form nor comeliness; and when we shall see him, there is no beauty that we should desire him.
3 He is despised and rejected of men; a man of sorrows, and acquainted with grief: and we hid as it were our faces from him; he was despised, and we esteemed him not.
4 Surely he hath borne our griefs, and carried our sorrows: yet we did esteem him stricken, smitten of God, and afflicted.
5 But he was wounded for our transgressions, he was bruised for our iniquities: the chastisement of our peace was upon him; and with his stripes we are healed.

Notice in verse 4, that the word "surely" is a covenant word. The word "surely" at the beginning of that scripture is saying to us, "I want you to get this. Beyond any shadow of any doubt, this is absolutely true." What's true? He hath borne our griefs, and carried our sorrows.

In Dr. Lesser's translation of the Hebrew he said, "Our diseases did He bear and our pains did He carry." Let me put that word "surely" in front of that. "Surely our diseases did He bear and surely our pains did He carry." He bore your disease and He carried your pain.

So you say, "Well then, why am I carrying it? Why am I sick?" Primarily Hosea 4:6 is the answer: *"My people are destroyed for a lack of knowledge."* If you don't know that Jesus bore your sickness and your disease, how can you believe Him for healing?

Jesus bore those sicknesses and pains, but He also sent His Word—His written Word—to be medicine to all our flesh. We have got a book of medicine here! And it doesn't cost us $7 a prescription or $22 a prescription. **Jesus paid the price with His blood!** And He said all people every where can come to Him in faith believing that He took those diseases, that He took those pains, and that His Word is medicine. They can take their prescription and be healed and made whole. I tell you **healing is for us today!**

GOD'S WORD IS TRUE

You don't have to be sick. You don't have to be weak. You don't have to die with disease in your body. Somebody says, "Well, how will I die?" Just go to sleep and wake up in heaven. We have got to receive our healing. We have got to receive it by faith in God's Word. God's Word is either true or it's not true. Jesus either bore our diseases or He didn't. He either bore our pains or He didn't.

Dr. Lesser's Bible is an accurate translation and it agrees with the next verse. Verse 5 says, *"But he was wounded for our transgressions..."* (Nobody doubts that. It amazes me how we can believe most of the scripture and then kick part of it out.) *"...he was bruised for our iniquities..."* (We believe that.) *"...the chastisement of our peace was upon him..."* (We believe that, but what about the last part?) *"...and with his stripes we are healed."* You can't just believe the first part and not believe the last part.

It amazes me that some say it is just spiritual stripes and spiritual healing. No. He is talking about ***Jehovah Rapha,*** the Lord that healeth me. That had to do with diseases and sicknesses, and the word ***rapha*** means "to cure or to be a physician or to make whole." It has to do with physical ailment. The devil doesn't want you well, but Jesus paid the price for you to be strong. The devil wants you sick and weakly, spending your money and wasting away, not happy, not feeling good, but that is totally opposite from what God desires for you.

THE BLOOD CLEANSES AND HEALS

God said above all things, beloved, I want you to prosper and I want you to be in health. So if we are going to believe that He was wounded for our transgressions—and we do, and that He was bruised for our iniquities—and we do, and the chastisement of our peace was upon Him, then why not believe that we are healed by His stripes? We have to come to this conclusion, beloved, that **the same blood that was shed for the remission of our sins was shed for the healing of our bodies.**

HEBREWS 9:19-22

19 For when Moses had spoken every precept to all the people according to the law, he took the blood of calves and of goats, with water, and scarlet wool, and hyssop, and sprinkled both the book, and all the people,

20 Saying, This is the blood of the testament which God hath enjoined unto you.

21 Moreover he sprinkled with blood both the tabernacle, and all the vessels of the ministry.

22 And almost all things are by the law purged with blood; and without shedding of blood is no remission.

Now, he's talking there about a comparison between the blood that was shed in the Old Testament and the blood that was shed in the New Testament. And he goes on to say that Jesus has put away sin by the shedding of His blood. We understand that and receive that the blood of Jesus has destroyed sin's power in our lives. Let me tell you something: **the blood of Jesus destroyed the devil's power in your life and the blood of Jesus destroyed the power of sickness to rule in your life.**

That word "enjoined" in verse 20 is such a powerful word. It means "to command to you, to be ordained for you, to be made binding upon you, or to be prescribed for you." The blood of Jesus is God's prescription for man. In the shedding of that blood is not only forgiveness of your sins, but also healing for your body. I am telling you **Jesus is your healer.** Jesus wants you well today. And if you will believe the Word and feed upon scriptures like Proverbs 4:20-22, that Word will become life.

LIFE IN THE WORD

Remember the scripture says life is in the blood so that Word will become life. It will produce life because the blood provided the Word. It will produce life in you and it will be medicine to all your flesh. God's prescription is healing for your body. Take God's Word and believe it. Reach out and begin to praise Him and thank Him for it.

> **ROMANS 10:17**
> **17 So then faith cometh by hearing, and hearing by the word of God.**

The more you hear that healing is for you, the more faith will come. And the more faith comes, the sooner you will be able to reach out and say, "I believe. It's mine. God is my healer. Jesus wants me well." And you will rise up out of that sickness, out of that weakness, out of that painful situation, and give God glory and praise forever.

Healing truly belongs to you. Remember, God says His people perish for a lack of knowledge. We are going to endeavor to go through the Word line upon line, sharing scripture with you that will build faith into your heart for healing because according to God's Word, healing is for you.

LESSON 5: GOD'S SALVATION

"The LORD *is my light and my salvation; whom shall I fear?..."* (Psalm 27:1) Did you ever think about this? The word "salvation" both in the Hebrew and the Greek means a lot more than saved from sin. It means "to be saved, delivered, preserved, prospered, and made whole." So that word alone will tell us that physical healing is in God's plan of redemption for our life. When you say, "I'm saved," the Greek word ***sozo,*** you are saying, "I'm saved, I'm delivered, I'm preserved, I'm prosperous, and I'm made whole. Hallelujah, glory to God, I'm healed!" So thank God healing belongs to us today.

FAITH COMES BY HEARING

ROMANS 10:17
17 So then faith cometh by hearing, and hearing by the word of God.

Faith for anything comes by hearing and hearing by the Word of God. How did you get saved or born again? You heard. Somebody told you about Jesus. Somebody told you about the death, burial and resurrection of Jesus—that He died for your sins. And what did you do? You believed it and you acted upon it. You confessed Jesus as your Lord and became born again. You became a Christian.

Well, the same faith that got you saved will get you healed. And the reason it will is because in the plan of redemption, the same blood that was shed to forgive your sins provided healing for your body. Remember Isaiah's report? Isaiah was looking to Calvary and he said, *" Surely he hath borne our griefs, and carried our sorrows..."* Dr. Lesser's Bible says "Surely He bore our diseases and carried our pains." Now that's a more accurate translation. The next verse says,

ISAIAH 53:5
5 But he was wounded for our transgressions, he was bruised for our iniquities: the chastisement of our peace was upon him; and with his stripes we are healed.

We are healed. He was looking forward to Calvary—to the death, burial, and resurrection. *"...with his stripes we are healed."* Now no one that knows the Lord denies that he was wounded for our transgressions. If you didn't believe that, how in the world could you ever get saved? He was bruised for our guilt and iniquity. You don't have to be guilty as a Christian. Condemnation doesn't have to rule over you. Bless God, you made mistakes before you were saved, and you've made some after you were saved, but the blood of Jesus is still greater than your mistakes. The Bible also says in the same scripture that He provided peace for us. He is ***Jehovah Shalom,*** our well being, our prosperity, and our peace of mind. And, then, by His stripes we are healed.

REVIEW

This scripture contains the fact that healing belongs to us. So believe it, receive it and operate in it. Let's review what we have discussed here in these last few lessons. It is important that we hear and hear and hear, and review and review so that it gets solidified in our thinking. In our hearts, and in our lives. After all, one of the best ways to learn is by review.

PSALM 107:19
19 Then they cry unto the LORD in their trouble, and he saveth them out of their distresses.

Are you crying to the Lord in your trouble? Are you looking to Him for healing today? Believe in God to raise you up and make you well and strong. It is provided for you, but you've got to ask for it and believe it. When you cry to the Lord, he will save you out of your distress. And sickness, as we know, can cause a lot of distress.

PSALM 107:20
20 He sent his word, and healed them, and delivered them from their destructions.

He sent His Word and healed them. Now why would God do that for someone in the Old Testament and not do it for you in the New Testament? We have a better covenant built on better promises (Hebrews 8:6). If God sent His Word and healed them, then there is healing for you today and there is deliverance from destruction. He said one key thing you should do in verse 21.

PSALM 107:21
21 Oh that men would praise the LORD for his goodness, and for his wonderful works to the children of men!

Have you been praising God for His healing power and for healing you? That is an act of faith in itself, isn't it? When you can say, "Thank you, Lord for healing me," and you don't have any physical symptoms in your body that you are healed, but you have scriptural assurance through the Word that healing is yours, then that is an act of faith. God wants you well. God is good and healing is an act of His goodness and compassion.

I believe God wants people well more often than people want to be well. Because He sent His Son—the dearest thing that He had. He provided forgiveness from sin and healing for our bodies. **Healing is an act of God's goodness.** God is good. You should say that to yourself over and over, "God is good." He did not make you sick. He did not put sickness on your child or you. Sickness is a work of the devil that is trying to kill, steal, and destroy you. But God wants you well. He said to praise Him for His goodness and His wonderful works. Therefore, healing is an act of God's goodness and it is a demonstration of His wonderful works. God does wonderful things and **healing is a wonderful thing!**

STAY HEALTHY: WALK IN LOVE

EXODUS 15:26
26 And said, If thou wilt diligently hearken to the voice of the LORD thy God, and wilt do that which is right in his sight, and wilt give ear to his commandments, and keep all his statutes, I will put none of these diseases upon thee, which I have brought upon the Egyptians: for I am the LORD that healeth thee.

Well, right there it tells you that God is not putting disease upon people. The word "put" is a causative verb and should be translated as "allow." "I will allow none of these diseases to be upon thee." Because if you are walking in God's statutes, then He is not going to allow disease on you.

That answers a question why disease comes sometimes. Because we get out of God's laws and statutes. For instance, the greatest commandment that we have is to love the Lord our God with all our heart, mind, soul, and strength; and to love our neighbors as ourselves. The love commandment becomes the greatest commandment of all.

We know that unforgiveness can make you sick. It can open a door. If you hold resentment and bitterness and hatred—even if you've been mistreated and the other person was totally wrong—if you harbor that resentment, then that will open or can open a door for sickness and disease. What He is saying here is, "I'm not going to allow it on you." In essence, you allow it on yourself if you walk in disobedience.

We have got to understand that there are natural laws that can be broken and that can open a door to sickness and disease. You have got to take care of yourself. But we must understand that there is an evil spirit out there called the devil who wants to steal, kill, and destroy you. He majors in this stuff. He wants to bring sickness on you so he can cause you to be ineffective, inoperative, and unproductive. He wants you to be eventually destroyed by it.

We have got to come to grips with this thing. Sickness is not God's will for our lives. If it is then why would He lay it on His Son? Why would He say that by Jesus' stripes we are healed? I'll just tell you the truth: Sickness is no more God's will for our lives than sin is. Jesus dealt with both problems.

God said, "I'm not going to allow it on you. You stay in my love commandment, you keep my statutes, and the devil won't be able to touch you." Then He said, "I am the Lord that healeth thee. I'm not the one making you sick. I'm the one making you well! I'm the one that brought you the deliverance and the healing." God is your friend. God is your solution. God is your answer. He is ***Jehovah Rapha,*** the Lord that healeth thee. Remember the literal translation of ***Jehovah Rapha*** is "I exist eternally to thoroughly make you whole."

Part of God's reason for existence is to bring total healing to you and deliverance and freedom and to bring you into divine health . Part of the reason He sent His son was for your physical well being. It is time for you to knock sickness right between the eyes, run the devil out, and claim your deliverance based on the Word of God!

THE WORD MADE FLESH

JOHN 1:1,3,4

1 In the beginning was the Word, and the Word was with God, and the Word was God.

3 All things were made by him; and without him was not any thing made that was made.

4 In him was life; and the life was the light of men.

JOHN 1:14

14 And the Word was made flesh, and dwelt among us, (and we beheld his glory, the glory as of the only begotten of the Father,) full of grace and truth.

The Word is a person. Grace and truth came by Jesus Christ, and so Jesus is the Word of God. The book of Revelation describes Him: He is on a white horse and His name is the Word of God. Jesus is the Word that was with God in the beginning—that was God. All things were made by Him and He is the Word made flesh.

We see in Psalm107:20 that He sent His Word and healed them and Jesus is the Word. Then part of the reason why Jesus was sent was to bring healing. There is healing in the Word.

When we use the word "Word" we are talking about Jesus, the living Word and also the Bible, the written Word. There's healing in the Word. Jesus provided it and then this written Word becomes a connection for us to enter into the provision that he made.

PROVERBS 4:20

20 My son, attend to my words; incline thine ear unto my sayings.

We talked about the importance of giving God's Word first place and listening to or hearing the Word. See yourself well through the Word. Because many people are surrounded by just the natural report, they never see beyond that sickness. Did you know that part of the reason the children of Israel did not cross the Jordan River into the promise of God was that they could not see beyond that river? They couldn't see beyond that wilderness. They couldn't see themselves possessing the land.

Canaan is a type of God's promise to you. Canaan could represent healing for you. You have got to see yourself beyond that Jordan River. It may look like a big giant—that's what they saw. They said, "We can't take it, we can't see ourselves winning. We don't believe it. We are full of fear and doubt." But Joshua and Caleb said, "Let's go at once and possess the land!" They had faith and they could see themselves on the other side of that Jordan. As far as they were concerned, it was already done. They said, "God has given us this land—let's go for it!"

God has given you the land of healing and health. The land of sickness does not belong to you and you've got to rise up and say, "Bless God! I can see myself well! I can see myself passing over to the land of healing!" Look at yourself through the Word. If you'll do that, it will stay in your heart. **Faith is of the heart.** That is a good thing to remember. It is a spiritual force. Faith is of the heart and it comes from the Word.

TAKE GOD'S MEDICINE

As you hear and give attention to the Word, it fills your heart with faith. For His Word is life and medicine to all your flesh. You can take God's Word daily just like you take a prescription from a doctor. You take that pill and you put it in your mouth, and drink it down with water. You take that scripture and you say, "God said in Exodus 15:26 that He is the Lord that healeth me. And in Matthew 8:17, He took my infirmities and bore my sicknesses. I put that medicine in my mouth. I acknowledge it. I confess it. I receive it. I believe it. I drink it down with praise. I drink it down with prayer. I drink it down with the Holy Ghost." You begin to praise Him for your healing.

As you praise Him, you're taking that medicine and it begins to work in you. You've got to take prescriptions for an extended period of time for them to be effective in your body. God's Word will work the same way. Some folks want to *try* it. "Well, I tried that and it didn't help me any." Why don't you take the whole bottle? Take the whole thing before you just give up. God's Word is medicine to all of your flesh.

Hosea 4:6 said His people perish for a lack of knowledge. That is why we are trying to bring knowledge and help to you concerning the Word of God and healing. It will be a tremendous blessing and strength to your life.

It is so important that you hear the Word so that your faith will be stirred and healing can come. By faith, begin to thank God for your healing. Go to His Word, look up those scriptures, take your medicine, drink it down with praise and prayer. You are going to see your body get stronger and stronger because healing is for you.

If you stir your heart to praise God and to thank Him for His goodness and His wonderful works, healing power will flow into you and make you every whit whole. Healing comes from Jesus. Take your medicine. Get in the Word and meditate on it. It will build your faith and healing will come forth speedily.

NOTES

LESSON 6: GOD HONORS FAITH

GOD IS WITH US

Praise God for Jesus. Thank God that we can dance in our fire or that we can rejoice in the time of tribulation. You know why? Because there's somebody with us. If you know Jesus today, then He is with you. He doesn't forsake you when the going gets tough. He doesn't run away when the problems arise. He said, "I'll be with you even unto the end of the age."

You may be in a hospital bed someplace, but I want you to know that if you know the Lord, He is with you. If you'll just begin to thank Him and worship Him and rejoice in Him, then He will begin a work in you that will produce absolute miracle-working power.

In Acts chapter 10, Peter has been summoned by Cornelius and God has worked in both cases. An angel appeared to Cornelius and told him where to go to find Peter. And then Peter had a vision where God told him not to call unclean what God has hallowed or sanctified. This was the first time that the gospel was preached to the Gentiles.

So Peter went to Cornelius' house and he began to share the gospel with him. The Word says that Peter opened his mouth and he said, "Of a truth I perceive that God is no respecter of persons."

GOD IS NO RESPECTER OF PERSONS

God is no respecter of persons today. If He has ever healed anybody, He will heal you. **He has obligated Himself to honor your faith.** And your faith in Jesus can make you whole and well. He is no respecter of persons, but He is a respecter of faith.

For example, salvation is provided for everybody. Every person on this planet has a right to be saved. But salvation only comes to those who release their faith in the death, burial and resurrection of Jesus Christ.

God doesn't care what your background is or where you are from or what your problem is or how low of a gutter you've been in. When you cry out and say, "Jesus, save me, come into my life, and forgive me of my sins," you will get God's attention and salvation will come. The same thing is true regarding healing. Healing belongs to everybody, but not everybody receives it. But according to the scripture, the same time Jesus purchased our freedom from Satan's power, he purchased our freedom from sickness and disease.

God is no respecter of persons. If He's done it for one, He will do it for all. He will do it for you because it is in His Word.

So Peter went on and talked to them about the gospel and summed it up in Acts 10:38.

ACTS 10:38
38 How God anointed Jesus of Nazareth with the Holy Ghost and with power: who went about doing good, and healing all that were oppressed of the devil; for God was with him.

Peter said this is God's message: *"How God anointed Jesus of Nazareth with the Holy Ghost and power..."*

JESUS, THE ANOINTED ONE

Jesus was anointed by God with the Holy Ghost and with power. Thank God, that is good news. **Jesus is the Anointed One. And in His anointing there is healing power.**

There was healing power when He walked the shores of Galilee, and there is healing power in His anointing today and it is available to you. If you can believe that God anointed Jesus to heal you, then you can receive a miracle. That healing power will work for you today just like it worked back then.

"How God..." so God is the source of this anointing. What did He do? He *"anointed Jesus of Nazareth with the Holy Ghost and with power."* What for? *"who went about doing good and healing all that were oppressed of the devil..."* It says right there that God anointed Jesus to go around the countryside doing good.

HEALING IS GOOD

Remember I said to you that healing is one of God's goodnesses? Healing is a good thing, wouldn't you say so? Sickness is bad. Somebody said, "I've been sick, and I've been well, and well is a lot better." That's true because sickness is bad and healing is good. Something that steals and robs and destroys you is not from God. Healing is a mercy. Forgiveness is a mercy. Both have been provided for us by our merciful God.

Jesus was anointed by God with the Holy Ghost and with power. He went about doing good. What kind of good did He do? Healing. Healing is described in the scripture as something that is good. We sing that song, "God is so good..." and He is so good. I want you to know that healing is good. The same God that brought you the goodness of forgiveness will bring you the goodness of healing.

He went about doing good and healing all. **He healed all that believed.** He healed all that would allow Him to.

You remember when Jesus went into His hometown in Mark, chapter 6, He began to preach to them the same message He had preached in other places. And in the other places where He preached that Word, faith rose in the people's hearts and they received miracles, demons were cast out, healings took place, and God's workings were going on. Because the people received it. In Nazareth when they heard Him preach they said, "Who is he? We know him. He's the carpenter's boy. We know his brothers and sisters. Where did he get this knowledge?" The Bible said they were offended at Him. In other words, they did not receive His ministry. They did not receive His message.

FAITH ACTIVATES THE POWER

Because they didn't receive it, the Bible says, *"And he could there do no mighty work, save that he laid his hands upon a few sick folk, and healed them"* (Mark 6:5). It didn't say He would not do it, it said He could not do it. It said He laid His hands on a few sick folks with minor ailments. He healed a few headaches and a few minor ailments. That's all He could do in that city because their unbelief short-circuited the power of God.

In another case, in Mark 5, the little woman with the issue of blood had her faith plugged into the power of God. She believed the messenger, she believed the message, she believed in His anointing, and she believed that healing was hers. She reached out and plugged in and she got the power. But in His hometown, the power was short-circuited. There He could do no mighty works.

Some folks have the idea that if God wants them healed, then He can just heal them anytime He wants to. Let me ask you this, how come God just didn't save you anytime He wanted to? It took an act of your will to receive Jesus as your Lord and Savior. Was it God's will for you to be saved? Sure! The book of Timothy said it is God's will that **all men be saved.** Yet we know that some men are not saved. They do not receive what Jesus did for them. But it is God's will that all be saved.

If it is God's will for all to be saved, do we dare believe that it's God's will for all to be healed? I say we do. It is in the same covenant. It was bought by the same blood. It was purchased by the same sacrifice. It comes from the same God.

GOD WANTS YOU WELL

This scripture in Acts 10:38 says, He went about healing *all.* God's will is for all to be well. If God wants all to be well, then surely He wants you to be well. Some people don't know that. They've been told that God is not sure whether He wants them well or not. They have been told that God is punishing them, that He put sickness on them to teach them a lesson. You can't back that up with scripture. Sickness, disease, infirmities, and trials come, but **Jesus is our deliverer and it is His will that all be made well.** Will everybody receive their healing? Probably not. Not everyone receives their salvation. But nevertheless, it is God's will to heal.

You can receive your healing. Dare to believe it. Say, "It's mine. I believe it. Jesus wants me well." Why wouldn't He want you well? He is the God of love, mercy, compassion, grace, and glory. He is your heavenly Father. Do any of you parents want your children sick? I don't think so. So our heavenly Father doesn't want His children sick. He wants you well. "Then why am I sick?" There could be different reasons, but the number one reason is a lack of knowledge. *"My people are destroyed for lack of knowledge…"* (Hosea 4:6). That is why I want to share with you scriptures that prove the fact that healing is part of the gospel.

Jesus went about healing all that were oppressed of the devil, for God was with Him. Let me ask you a question. If Jesus went about healing all who were oppressed of the devil then, isn't it His will to heal all that are oppressed of the devil now?

The Bible calls sickness satanic oppression. In other words, it comes from the enemy. It doesn't come from heaven. There is no sickness in heaven.

REVELATION 21:4

4 **And God shall wipe away all tears from their eyes; and there shall be no more death, neither sorrow, nor crying, neither shall there be any more pain: for the former things are passed away.**

REVELATION 22:3

3 **And there shall be no more curse: but the throne of God and of the Lamb shall be in it; and his servants shall serve him:**

No more curse. Sickness is not in heaven. God didn't send it. Galatians 3:13 says, *"Christ hath redeemed us from the curse of the law…"* Sickness was a curse then and it is a curse now. It is part of the curse that won't be in heaven and it is part of the curse that doesn't belong in our life. Thank God, He wants you well!

CAUSES OF INFIRMITY

"Satanic oppression" simply means that the devil is involved in sickness and disease. Sometimes evil spirits can be causing it.

LUKE 13:11
11 And, behold, there was a woman which had a spirit of infirmity eighteen years, and was bowed together, and could in no wise lift up herself.

So this woman was bowed over and the Bible said there was a spirit of infirmity that was causing it. An evil spirit had attached itself to her body and was actually crippling this woman. What happened? When Jesus saw her he said, *"Woman, thou art loosed from thine infirmity,"* (verse 12).

He broke the power of that evil spirit and set the woman free. Then, *"he laid his hands on her: and immediately she was made straight, and glorified God,"* (verse 13). Now we just read that God is no respecter of persons. If He wanted this little woman free who was bowed over and arthritic—or whatever the problem was—doesn't He want you free? Yes!

The Bible said the ruler of the synagogue got upset. He got mad because Jesus healed this woman on the Sabbath day.

LUKE 13:14
14 And the ruler of the synagogue answered with indignation, because that Jesus had healed on the sabbath day, and said unto the people, There are six days in which men ought to work: in them therefore come and be healed, and not on the sabbath day.

Can you believe that? Can you believe that somebody—a preacher—would rebuke this woman for receiving a miracle from the hand of the Lord? Yet I know today there are ministers that stand up and tell their churches that healing is not for today.

I don't know how you can say that and read the Bible. God is the God of Abraham, Isaac and Jacob. The God and Father of our Lord Jesus Christ. He provided healing for His people in the Old Testament. He is still ***Jehovah Rapha*** today in the New Testament, and healing belongs to us.

LUKE 13:15, 16
15 The Lord then answered him, and said, Thou hypocrite, doth not each one of you on the sabbath loose his ox or his ass from the stall, and lead him away to watering?

16 **And ought not this woman, being a daughter of Abraham, whom Satan hath bound, lo, these eighteen years, be loosed from this bond on the sabbath day?**

Jesus said, "If you're going to loose your oxen, I'm going to loose my children."

If you are one of His today, He wants you free from that infirmity. He wants you free from that satanic oppression. Now, not every sickness would necessarily have an evil spirit causing it. But nevertheless, sickness is of the devil's kingdom—not of God's kingdom.

JOHN 10:10
10 **The thief cometh not, but for to steal, and to kill, and to destroy: I am come that they might have life, and that they might have it more abundantly.**

Things that steal, kill and destroy are of the devil's kingdom. Sickness and disease fit into all three of these categories.

God wants you well. If God anointed Jesus with the Holy Ghost and power, and He went about with this anointing as the Anointed One and brought healing by it, then it must be God's will to heal. Because if it wasn't His will to heal, then why did the power that He anointed Jesus with produce healing? It did produce healing then, and it will produce it today. It is God's will for you to be well. God was the source of that healing anointing. God was behind it. God was involved in it.

REVELATION OF HEALING IN THE CHURCH

Did you ever think about this? Here is the early church in the book of Acts and this church is now about ten years old. They are just now finding out that the gospel was for the Gentiles as well—that all men could be saved. They are just now finding out that all people could be born again, receive the outpouring of the Holy Spirit and be healed. But did you ever notice this? Way back in the first chapters of Acts they were already ministering healing to people? **The revelation of healing came to the early church before the revelation of salvation to all men.**

The Jews were getting saved, people in Jerusalem were getting saved and getting healed. They understood that healing was part of the gospel. Healing has always been important to God. It has always been part of the gospel message. It has always been God's plan to bring healing to His people.

He brought it in the Old Testament, and He brought it in the New Testament. He brought it to the early church even before they knew the Gentiles could be saved. And as soon as the Gentiles got saved, one of the first things preached was *"How God anointed Jesus of Nazareth with the Holy Ghost and with power: who went about doing good, and healing all..."* (Acts 10:38). He said, "You guys can have your sins forgiven, your bodies made whole and become a temple of the Holy Ghost."

CLAIM YOUR HEALING NOW

You can do the same thing today. Jesus wants you well. Rise up and tell that devil to get his hands off your body. Claim your healing in Jesus' name. Take God's medicine—His Word—and believe that if God ever wanted anybody well and strong, He wants you well and strong today.

Receive that anointing today. Jesus is the Anointed One. He has been anointed by God Almighty with healing power. That healing power is for you. His grace and His mercy will come forth into your life today as you exercise your faith in the healing power of Jesus.

Do you know what to do? You simply say, "Lord, I believe. I believe that you want me well. I believe Jesus is anointed with healing power, and I believe I can have it now." Reach out with your hand of faith. Get a hold of God's rich promises and let healing power fill your life. Take authority over the devil and run him out of your family in Jesus' name.

LESSON 7:
CONFESS YOUR HEALING

It is a scriptural fact that Jesus wants you well. Look at the following scriptures.

MATTHEW 8:17
17 **That it might be fulfilled which was spoken by Esaias the prophet, saying, Himself took our infirmities, and bare our sicknesses.**

1 PETER 2:24
24 **Who his own self bare our sins in his own body on the tree, that we, being dead to sins, should live unto righteousness: by whose stripes ye were healed.**

So we can see that God has got something wonderful in store for you. Now let's go back to one of our key scriptures, Psalm 107:19:

PSALM 107:19
19 **Then they cry unto the LORD in their trouble, and he saveth them out of their distresses.**

Have you had any trouble lately? You know sickness is a lot of trouble. It affects your body, and brings trouble to your life. It can certainly cause distress and uneasiness. The Bible said when we cry unto the Lord, He delivers us out of our trouble.

PSALM 34:19
19 **Many are the afflictions of the righteous: but the LORD delivereth him out of them all.**

I'm glad He didn't stop with half of that scripture and just say many are the afflictions of the righteous. And that would be it. Thank God, when we go through the hard times, the rough times, the troubles, the sicknesses, and the problems of life, we can cry unto the Lord, and we have got this promise that says He delivers us out of them all.

So sickness certainly is a hard time. It's a struggle. It's trouble. It's a distressing time. It can rob you of your health, well being, finances, and your future. It is an enemy to the children of God and to the human race.

Notice verses 20 and 21 of Psalm 107:

PSALM 107:20,21
20 He sent his word, and healed them, and delivered them from their destructions.
21 Oh that men would praise the LORD for his goodness, and for his wonderful works to the children of men!

God said the reason He sent His Word was to bring healing and health and deliverance and strength. And then He caps it off by saying in verse 21 that healing is one of His goodnesses.

God wants to display his goodness to you today by bringing His healing power into your life and setting you free from sickness and disease. When you really look at it scripturally, the Bible says that God laid our sins upon Jesus, so the work has been done. It is our faith in God's Word that causes us to reach out and grab a hold of that promise and receive it unto ourselves and begin to praise God for it and thank Him that it's true. Healing is a goodness that comes from God.

THE PROVISION OF HEALTH

Our heavenly Father made great provision for you when He sent Jesus to the cross. Through the death, burial, and resurrection of Jesus Christ, we can have salvation for our souls and healing for our bodies. He sent His Word and healed them. There is healing power in the Word.

JOHN 1:14
14 And the Word was made flesh, and dwelt among us, (and we beheld his glory, the glory as of the only begotten of the Father,) full of grace and truth.

Jesus is the Word that was made flesh and dwelt among us. God's spoken Word has always contained healing power. When He sent His Word, He sent it to heal. That word is ***rapha,*** which means "to heal, to be a physician, to doctor, to be made whole." So God sent His Word in the Old Testament to heal His people and God sent His Son, the Word, in the New Testament to heal His people.

Jesus has come and provided healing for us. He is the Word of God today. Jesus is the living Word and the Bible is the written Word. The Bible becomes a healing agent. The Bible becomes a healing Word. Just like Jesus is the healing Word. He took our sicknesses.

Proverbs 4 says God's Word is like medicine.

PROVERBS 4:22
22 **For they are life unto those that find them, and health** [or medicine] **to all their flesh.**

Let the Word produce faith in you. As that faith is produced, it will reach out and grab hold of God's promise concerning healing and make you whole.

Remember the little woman with the issue of blood?

MARK 5:25-34
25 **And a certain woman, which had an issue of blood twelve years,**
26 **And had suffered many things of many physicians, and had spent all that she had, and was nothing bettered, but rather grew worse,**
27 **When she had heard of Jesus, came in the press behind, and touched his garment.**
28 **For she said, If I may touch but his clothes, I shall be whole.**
29 **And straightway the fountain of her blood was dried up; and she felt in her body that she was healed of that plague.**
30 **And Jesus, immediately knowing in himself that virtue had gone out of him, turned him about in the press, and said, Who touched my clothes?**
31 **And his disciples said unto him, Thou seest the multitude thronging thee, and sayest thou, Who touched me?**
32 **And he looked round about to see her that had done this thing.**
33 **But the woman fearing and trembling, knowing what was done in her, came and fell down before him, and told him all the truth.**

34 And he said unto her, Daughter, thy faith hath made thee whole; go in peace, and be whole of thy plague.

It was that little woman's faith that reached out and touched His garment that caused that healing power to flow into her life from Jesus, who is the living Word. Jesus said, "Your faith has made you whole."

GET IN THE WORD

I want to build up your faith in God's Word. Because if that woman's faith could make her whole, then your faith in God's promise will make you whole. It's like there is a storehouse already full of healing and God is just waiting for you and me or anyone to just tap into it with our faith. You can do it if you'll get into the Word. Let's build our faith up so that we can make a connection to receive that healing power.

PROVERBS 2:20-22
20 My son, attend to my words; incline thine ear unto my sayings.
21 Let them not depart from thine eyes; keep them in the midst of thine heart.
22 For they are life unto those that find them, and health to all their flesh.

God's Word is a good report and this report will make you well. Verse 22 says His words are life. The word "life" in the New Testament is the Greek word zoe, meaning "absolute life or the God-kind of life." It is the kind of life that overcomes every kind of sickness. God's Word is life to all that find it. You've got to spend some time finding it. Let God's Word begin to build your faith for it is life—the God-kind of life—absolute life.

The King James says, "health to all their flesh." The margin of my Bible says "medicine" to all their flesh. So what is that saying? If you take God's Word into your life, it will produce healing and health. Thank God for the Word. There's power in the Word of God. In Proverbs, He said His words would produce life in all that find them. Jesus is a life-giver. The Word of God is a life-giver. As you hear the Word and get into the Word, those scriptures will begin to produce life. Faith will begin to rise up and healing will be the result.

HEBREWS 4:12,13
12 For the word of God is quick, and powerful, and sharper than any twoedged sword, piercing even to the dividing asunder of soul and spirit, and of the joints and marrow, and is a discerner of the thoughts and intents of the heart.
13 Neither is there any creature that is not manifest in his sight: but all things are naked and opened unto the eyes of him with whom we have to do.

He said there's not one thing that God's Word won't affect. God's Word covers every aspect of our life. But we are talking specifically about the promises of healing. He said there's not one creature that is hid, not one circumstance that it doesn't cover, not one situation that God can't answer. His Word will produce sufficient faith to see us through and cause us to overcome.

HEBREWS 4:14
14 Seeing then that we have a great high priest, that is passed into the heavens, Jesus the Son of God, let us hold fast our profession.

You have a great high priest. Who is He? He is Jesus! Who is Jesus? The Word! What does the Word do? It makes you whole. It is medicine to all your flesh.

HOLD FAST TO YOUR CONFESSION

You have a high priest today and he is in His high priestly office. He never sleeps. He never slumbers. He is watching over His Word to perform it. He is watching over your life and He is just waiting for someone to believe His rich promises. Let us hold fast our confession or profession of faith. We are talking about holding fast to the profession of faith for healing for our bodies. Jesus is our healer. His Word is our healer. He sent His Word to heal us. His Word is producing life in you today.

By faith claim your healing in Jesus' name because He paid for it.

1 PETER 2:24a
24 Who his own self bare our sins in his own body on the tree, that we, being dead to sins, should live unto righteousness:

Now we believe that. Anyone that's born again believes that Jesus bore our sins on Calvary. Look at the same scripture, the very last phrase:

1 PETER 2:24b
by whose stripes ye were healed.

The same Jesus that took our sins took our sicknesses. The same God that wants us to be dead to sin wants us to be dead to sickness.

Healing is great, but do you know what's better? **Divine health.** We've got to start where we are. Let's stir our faith to receive our healing. There's not one of us that hasn't had an opportunity to be sick or that hasn't been sick at one time or another.

DON'T ACCEPT CHRONIC FAMILY SICKNESS

You may be suffering today from a chronic situation—something that's been in your life or your family. God's got an answer for you today. Jesus came to set the captive free and to break the bondages of sin, sickness, disease, and poverty. He came to break that old history of cancer or kidney failure in your family. He came to give you hope for your future. He came to cause you to rise up and be well and strong and to tell the devil to get out of your family.

My mother had some problems with her kidneys in her later years. My dad developed a little kidney situation before he died. I found out that my mother's grandfather had a kidney problem. They said according to the history of the disease it skips a generation. It goes from grandfathers to granddaughters. When I heard that, I began to rebuke that spirit, cast it out of my life and the lives of my brothers and sisters and my children.

I'm not going to have it attacking my children because healing belongs to me in Jesus' name. I began to say, "My children will never have kidney failure. I won't have it and they won't have it because Jesus made us well." I began to pray for my children, my grandchildren and my great-grandchildren. I don't even have any grandchildren or great-grandchildren yet, but I'm praying for them anyway. This is a promise to a third and fourth generation even as many as the Lord our God has called.

I want to encourage you that that thing is broken today in the name of Jesus. It is broken by the Word of God and healing belongs to you. I don't care what someone in your family died from. I don't mean I'm not concerned that they died. I'm saying that it's not the issue when it comes to healing.

If Grandpa died of something, you don't have to die of it. If Mama or Daddy died of something, you don't have to die of it. Bless God, you can have your healing because Jesus provided it! His Word says it's so. And He says He's our high priest. He has gone into the heavens. He is there right now and He is watching over His Word to perform it.

The Bible says the eyes of the Lord run to and fro looking for someone that He can prove Himself strong in the behalf of (2 Chronicles 16:9). I believe He's found somebody today in you and in me. He is looking for those that will believe His promise.

Notice what He said,

HEBREWS 4:15
15 For we have not an high priest which cannot be touched with the feeling of our infirmities; but was in all points tempted like as we are, yet without sin.

Jesus knows how you feel. If anybody knows how you feel, Jesus does. If anybody knows what you've been through, Jesus does. If anybody knows what you're facing, Jesus does. Nobody else has walked in your shoes, but God Almighty sent His Son and He understands.

HEBREWS 4:16
16 Let us therefore come boldly unto the throne of grace, that we may obtain mercy, and find grace to help in time of need.

My dear friend, healing is one of God's mercies and it is yours today. Jesus is wanting to manifest that in your life. Grab hold of the fact that Jesus loves you and He took your sins and sicknesses. He is your high priest and He is waiting today for you to come boldly to His throne and receive the mercy of healing. If you'll do it, it will be yours.

Remember that beautiful gospel song, "He was nailed to the cross for me. He was nailed to the cross for me. On the cross crucified, for me He died. He was nailed to the cross for me." It goes on to talk about the death, burial, and resurrection of Jesus. We can sing that song with confidence about the forgiveness of our sins. And we can do the same thing with confidence for the healing of our bodies.

Forgiveness of sin is a mercy. Healing is a mercy. God's compassion is flowing to you today. Reach out and say, "It's mine. I take my healing now."

Get into the Word and read those rich promises. Let that Word begin to produce medicine for your body and healing will be the result.

LESSON 8:

JESUS IS THE SAME HEALER TODAY

Let's look at Matthew 9:35.

MATTHEW 9:35
35 **And Jesus went about all the cities and villages, teaching in their synagogues, and preaching the gospel of the kingdom, and healing every sickness and every disease among the people.**

Now back up a couple of verses.

MATTHEW 9:32,33
32 **As they went out, behold, they brought to him a dumb man possessed with a devil.**
33 **And when the devil was cast out, the dumb spake: and the multitudes marvelled, saying, It was never so seen in Israel.**

Verse 33 says He cast the devil out. That's what we need to do with the devil—cast him out! Jesus defeated him for us and whipped him, but we have to use our authority and cast him out.

This same Jesus that worked miracles is still working them today because He is the Anointed of the Lord. He has the anointing to heal. He went about all the cities and villages and taught in their synagogues. He preached the gospel of the good news of the kingdom. Thank God, the gospel of the kingdom includes healing. Healing is good. It is good news. And it is one of God's goodnesses.

Jesus healed every disease and every sickness. There was not one disease or one sickness among the people that was not subject to the healing power of Jesus of Nazareth. He is the Word of God and there is still no sickness or disease today that is not subject to His healing power. It doesn't matter what they call it, it is still subject to the name of Jesus. It is subject to the anointing of Jesus and it is subject to the Word of Almighty God.

MEDICINE TO ALL YOUR FLESH

It is no wonder that Proverbs said His Word would be medicine to all your flesh. You can take God's Word and begin to put it in your heart, in your mouth, in your ears, and before your eyes, and as you drink it down with praise, it will affect all your flesh.

Every sickness and disease is subject to the Word of God and the name of Jesus. AIDS, cancer, tuberculosis, arthritis, inflammation in the joints, organ disease, liver disease, heart failure—they all have to bow to the name of Jesus. Every disease was subject then, and every disease is subject today.

So no matter what you are diagnosed with, there is a remedy. There is a fountain filled with blood, drawn from Immanuel's veins, and sinners plunged beneath that flood lose all their guilty stains. The same blood that provided salvation from sin also provides salvation from sickness.

Jesus went about preaching, teaching and healing. I believe that's a good way to go about the ministry of Christ today. Keep preaching, teaching, healing and believing God.

Now let's look back at Matthew.

> **MATTHEW 9:36-38**
> **36 But when he saw the multitudes, he was moved with compassion on them, because they fainted, and were scattered abroad, as sheep having no shepherd.**
> **37 Then saith he unto his disciples, The harvest truly is plenteous, but the labourers are few;**
> **38 Pray ye therefore the Lord of the harvest, that he will send forth labourers into his harvest.**

Now He was saying, pray, and we understand this. We preach it, teach it, and believe it. He said, pray that God would send forth laborers into this harvest field where the sheep are scattered, having no shepherd, so that the message of salvation from their sin can be brought to them.

Primarily, when people use this scripture that is what they are praying for, "Lord, send a laborer to my child, my family, this nation, or my home. Send me. Let me preach the gospel of salvation so men and women can believe it and be saved and go to heaven when they die." That is a valid message and it is the most important one when it comes to heaven or hell because without being born again, you can't go to heaven.

Did you ever realize that the same Jesus that had compassion on the sinner had compassion on the sick? The Bible says He had compassion on the multitude and healed the sick. The same compassionate Jesus that wants you saved wants you well. All through the Gospels—Matthew, Mark, Luke and John—a picture is painted of a compassionate Jesus that forgave sin and healed the sick. And He is alive today.

JESUS: OUR COMPASSIONATE HIGH PRIEST

Now let me ask you something. Has Jesus lost any of His compassion? I don't think so.

HEBREWS 4:14, 15

14 Seeing then that we have a great high priest, that is passed into the heavens, Jesus the Son of God, let us hold fast our profession.

15 For we have not an high priest which cannot be touched with the feeling of our infirmities; but was in all points tempted like as we are, yet without sin.

That is compassion. Jesus has compassion for people in their loneliness, sin or sickness. The Bible says we have a high priest that can easily be touched. So, if anything, He is more compassionate today—not less. His compassion may not have changed as far as He is concerned, but it has certainly become more available to the human race because of His death, burial and resurrection. That flung heaven's door of mercy wide open for the forgiveness of sin, the healing of your body, and the restoration of your mind.

We have a compassionate Jesus today. He is looking on your situation and He has compassion on you. He is just waiting for you to rise up in faith and dare to believe. Reach out and receive that compassion today.

So, according to Hebrews 4:14,15, we have to hold fast to our confession, and then we've got to come boldly to the throne of grace. Why? To obtain mercy and find help in the time of need. Now why don't we do that concerning sickness? We come boldly to the throne of grace concerning salvation. In many churches we have an altar call or we'll ask somebody to pray with us. We will pray believing without a shadow of a doubt that God hears those prayers and forgives those sins. So, why can't we simply transfer that faith and apply it to sickness and disease?

The same Jesus that was compassionate over our sins is compassionate over our sickness. He said to come boldly to the throne of grace to obtain mercy. I think a lot of people have thought that mercy only meant forgiveness of sins. But really, throughout the Bible the sick cried out for mercy for healing the same way they cried out for mercy for forgiveness.

Case and point: When blind Bartimaeus cried out to Jesus on the roadside, he needed healing—he needed a miracle. You know what He said? He cried out with a loud voice, "Jesus, thou son of David have mercy on me!" (Mark 10). Healing, in his thinking was a mercy. Well, it's a mercy in God's thinking too.

The Bible says if you can come boldly to the throne of grace and get your sins forgiven, you can come boldly to the throne of grace and receive healing for your body. Just bow down before God and say, "In the name of Jesus, I receive healing for my body." Boldly believe it is yours and then thank God for it. Praise Him and give Him glory for it. That is when the miracle takes place.

TEN LEPERS HEALED

LUKE 17:11-14
11 And it came to pass, as he went to Jerusalem, that he passed through the midst of Samaria and Galilee.
12 And as he entered into a certain village, there met him ten men that were lepers, which stood afar off:
13 And they lifted up their voices, and said, Jesus, Master, have mercy on us.

14 And when he saw them, he said unto them, Go show yourselves unto the priests. And it came to pass, that, as they went, they were cleansed.

These lepers were crying for the mercy of healing. "Have mercy on us!" In their minds, the same mercy that would forgive their sins would heal their bodies. (It ought to be the same way in our minds.) Jesus said, "Go show yourself to the priest," and as they went, as they acted on His Word, they were healed.

LUKE 17:15-19
15 And one of them, when he saw that he was healed, turned back, and with a loud voice glorified God,
16 And fell down on his face at his feet, giving him thanks: and he was a Samaritan.
17 And Jesus answering said, Were there not ten cleansed? but where are the nine?
18 There are not found that returned to give glory to God, save this stranger.
19 And he said unto him, Arise, go thy way: thy faith hath made thee whole.

Notice what He said to this one. He said to this man, "Arise, go your way. Your faith has made you whole." There were ten cleansed, but there was only one that was made whole.

Everything that had ever been damaged in his body by that disease was wiped out by the power of God all because he took the time to give God the praise. **There is power in praising God!**

If you can get a hold of the fact that healing belongs to you, just like forgiveness of sins, you could come boldly to that throne of grace and receive it. Then you begin to praise God for it and let Him work the work.

HOW LONG DOES IT TAKE?

You say, "How long does it take for the manifestation?" I don't know. Sometimes it comes quicker that others. You say, "Do I keep taking my medicine or do I quit?" Well, I would take whatever natural medicine you've got that can help you. Your faith is not in taking the medicine. Your faith is in the Word of

God. So as you take your medicine, begin praising God for your healing. Come boldly, receive it, thank Him for it, call it done, and begin to praise Him for it. Your faith in His promise will make you whole.

Jesus is still healing today and healing belongs to you. Healing is one of God's goodnesses to you and His compassions fail not. As you begin to acknowledge that, confess that, believe and receive that, then God will make it good in your life.

JEREMIAH 1:12
12 Then said the LORD unto me, Thou hast well seen: for I will hasten my word [I am watching over My Word]**to perform it.**

Praise Him for your healing. Believe it's yours. Stand on His rich promises and He will make it good!

LESSON 9: THE ANOINTING IS AVAILABLE TO YOU

ANOINTED WITH POWER TO HEAL

ACTS 10:38
38 How God anointed Jesus of Nazareth with the Holy Ghost and with power: who went about doing good, and healing all that were oppressed of the devil; for God was with him.

Sickness is a satanic oppression. The devil is involved in making people sick one way or another. I know sometimes we can do silly things and break natural laws and make ourselves sick, but the source of sickness and disease is not from heaven and not from God. The devil uses that to destroy the body, the mind, and the finances of people.

Jesus went about healing all that were oppressed of the devil for God was with Him. Now , we ask the question, if Jesus went about healing all that were oppressed of the devil then, why isn't He going about healing all that are oppressed of the devil now? He is! Jesus is the same yesterday, today and forever and the same Jesus lives in His body, the Church—the believer, the one who is born again.

Jesus said in Mark, chapter 16,

MARK 16:15-18
15 And he said unto them, Go ye into all the world, and preach the gospel to every creature.
16 He that believeth and is baptized shall be saved; but he that believeth not shall be damned.
17 And these signs shall follow them that believe; In my name shall they cast out devils; they shall speak with new tongues;
18 They shall take up serpents; and if they drink any deadly thing, it shall not hurt them; they shall lay hands on the sick, and they shall recover.

So, Jesus is still going about through His body healing people.

It is great to have somebody to lay hands on you, and we do that, of course, we believe in that, but you can rise up right where you are and say, "I believe I receive my healing!" You can claim it and then begin to praise Him for it. Because He is still a healing Jesus, He is still the Anointed of the Lord. He still has the healing anointing and it is available to you.

Therefore, you can have great confidence in that. Everything that Jesus does is good. He cast out devils, He taught in the synagogues, He preached the gospel of the kingdom and He healed the sick. Then He looked at the multitude and had compassion on them for the forgiveness of sin and the healing of their bodies. This is the same Jesus that we are talking about that wants you well.

JOHN 10:10
10 The thief cometh not, but for to steal, and to kill, and to destroy: I am come that they might have life, and that they might have it more abundantly.

Now the thief is the devil. He's the robber. He is the one trying to rob God's children of their blessings. Everything he does has that element in it. We can see then, that sickness steals from you . It steals your health, your well being, your finances, and your family. Anything that steals, kills or destroys is a work of the devil.

1 JOHN 3:8
8 He that committeth sin is of the devil; for the devil sinneth from the beginning. For this purpose the Son of God was manifested, that he might destroy the works of the devil.

RELATIONSHIP NOT RELIGION

We can readily apply that to sin. Jesus destroyed the works of sin in our lives and we become new creatures in Christ Jesus when we accept Him as our Lord and Savior. That is what makes Christianity different than all religions. Christianity is not really a religion. It's a relationship with a living God who loves you. But a religion says you've got to be good enough and do enough to reach God. It is man trying to reach God. Christianity is God reaching man in his fallen, sinful state and cleansing him, forgiving him, lifting him up in Christ, giving him a new life, and making him a new creature.

2 CORINTHIANS 5:17
17 Therefore if any man be in Christ, he is a new creature: old things are passed away; behold, all things are become new.

Have you been born again? Have you accepted Jesus? You know you can be a member of the first church of any denomination and still not be saved. It is not church membership that saves you—it is the new birth. It is calling on the name of Jesus out of a pure heart and asking Him to come into your life and make you a new creature. The new birth is the rebirth of your spirit. Jesus said you must be born again.

If you are not born again or sure of your eternal salvation, you can become a new creation today. Pray this prayer now: *"Dear Lord, I believe You died for me. I believe you arose from the dead. I receive Jesus as my Lord and Savior. I believe Jesus is my healer too. Amen."*

NOTES

LESSON 10: PRAISE YOUR WAY TO HEALING

I have found a way to get God's eyes to stop on me.

2 CHRONICLES 16:19
9 For the eyes of the LORD run to and fro throughout the whole earth, to show himself strong in the behalf of them whose heart is perfect toward him.

I tell you, I know how to get those eyes stopped. I know how to keep those eyes from bypassing my need. How? By going boldly to the throne of grace, receiving God's mercy, and worshipping and praising Him.

PRAISE OF FAITH

We talk about the prayer of faith, but did you know there is a praise of faith? I read something in a book just recently where this woman needed healing and deliverance for her daughter. She came and worshipped God. She got God's attention and the anointing was released. Her daughter was made whole.

The anointing is so strong, and God's Word is so powerful that it can go out into any given situation and cause it to be made new. That Word is going forth to you today.

Let's look back at some of our key scriptures.

PSALM 107:20
20 He sent his word, and healed them, and delivered them from their destructions.

ACTS 10:38
38 How God anointed Jesus of Nazareth with the Holy Ghost and with power: who went about doing good, and healing all that were oppressed of the devil; for God was with him.

Jesus is still doing good things today. He is still bringing healing to you today. Look at Luke 17.

LUKE 17:11
11 And it came to pass, as he went to Jerusalem, that he passed through the midst of Samaria and Galilee.
12 And as he entered into a certain village, there met him ten men that were lepers, which stood afar off:
13 And they lifted up their voices, and said, Jesus, Master, have mercy on us.

We find that all over the New Testament when people need healing or deliverance or forgiveness, they cried out for mercy. Did you know that the words "mercy" and "compassion" are translated the same? **Compassion can be translated as mercy and mercy can be translated as compassion.** The definition of "compassion" is "an eager yearning and willingness to help."

God's mercy is eagerly waiting for you to draw upon it to receive your healing. God's compassion is His willingness to heal you.

So these lepers were crying out for mercy for their healing. Leprosy was like the cancer of the day. It was eating away at their flesh. They were isolated and set apart from all their family members and they cried out, "Have mercy on us!"

LUKE 17:14
14 And when he saw them, he said unto them, Go show yourselves unto the priests. And it came to pass, that, as they went, they were cleansed.

So they had to act upon the Word to receive their healing. You are going to have to believe that Jesus is anointed. You are going to have to believe that healing is for you. You are going to have to believe that Jesus is our jubilee, that He came to bring us liberty in every sense of the word.

1 PETER 2:24
24 Who his own self bare our sins in his own body on the tree, that we, being dead to sins, should live unto righteousness: by whose stripes ye were healed.

God put the whole package together there for us in one verse so that you would know that Jesus, our jubilee, brought to us liberty and freedom from sin and also liberty and freedom from sickness.

So I think we can say boldly that sickness and disease do not belong to us. Healing is the children's bread. Healing belongs to anyone who will dare believe it!

WOMAN RECEIVES MERCY

We've looked at some of the examples of Jesus and His ministry and this healing power that went from Him. The same Jesus that walked the shores of Galilee is alive today with healing power available for us to receive.

MATTHEW 15: 21,22
21 Then Jesus went thence, and departed into the coasts of Tyre and Sidon.
22 And, behold, a woman of Canaan came out of the same coasts, and cried unto him, saying, Have mercy on me, O Lord, thou son of David; my daughter is grievously vexed with a devil.

Now here, this woman cried out for mercy for the deliverance for her daughter. For some reason, we have had this idea that mercy applied primarily to forgiveness of sins. But we all know that there are needs in our lives other than forgiveness.

So she cried out for mercy. Now notice what happened.

MATTHEW 15:23,24
23 But he answered her not a word. And his disciples came and besought him, saying, Send her away; for she crieth after us.
24 But he answered and said, I am not sent but unto the lost sheep of the house of Israel.

Jesus was sent with a mission. He had His mind made up that He was sent to the house of Israel first. The gospel is to the Jew first and also to the Greek. Thank God it belongs to everybody.

You know Jesus was giving this woman an opportunity to display her faith in a greater measure. And notice what happens.

MATTHEW 15:25
25 Then came she and worshipped him, saying, Lord, help me

26 But he answered and said, It is not meet to take the children's bread, and cast it to dogs.

This is where that statement comes from, "Healing is the children's bread," but actually it belongs to all of us that will believe.

MATTHEW 15:27,28
27 And she said, Truth, Lord: yet the dogs eat of the crumbs which fall from their masters' table.
28 Then Jesus answered and said unto her, O woman, great is thy faith: be it unto thee even as thou wilt.And her daughter was made whole from that very hour.

Now Jesus healed this woman's daughter and really, the daughter wasn't even any place to be seen. I can't find her in this story other than just in words.

Well, I am bringing the Word to you even though I'm not in your presence physically. But you know the Holy Spirit is there. Jesus is there. The Word is there and it is going forth to bring healing.

This daughter was made whole because of her mother's faith. She had faith in Jesus for healing. You can have the same faith in Jesus for healing today. If Jesus was ever anointed to heal, He is still anointed to heal today.

Now, notice that this woman tapped into this healing anointing through her worship and praise. I mean, she wasn't getting anywhere quick. She wasn't getting any answers or any help. The disciples couldn't help her and Jesus wasn't answering her.

Then she came to Him and began to worship and praise and magnify Him. God can never resist a worshipper. There is something about worshipping and praising Him that gets heaven's attention.

TAKE GOD'S MEDICINE FAITHFULLY

Healing is the children's bread. You have to reach out by faith and say, "It's mine. I have it now." Act upon it. Move your body. Get up out of bed, walk, stretch, believe. Do something in faith and watch what God will do.

Somebody always says, "Should I quit taking my medicine?" Well let me say this to you, God's Word is medicine. If you've got to take other medicine with it, fine! Take God's medicine and the other medicine, and do you know what will happen? If you take God's medicine faithfully, you will reach a place where you won't need any other medicine, because God's medicine is eternal medicine. It will affect your body and set you free. However, don't just throw your medicine away and do something presumptuously.

Act in faith. Remember, your faith is not in taking the medicine or in not taking the medicine. Your faith is in the Word of God. Act upon the Word. Move your body, make a confession, lift you hands, praise the Lord, and obey God. You will see the miracle working power come forth.

HEALING THERAPY

MATTHEW 8:16

16 When the even was come, they brought unto him many that were possessed with devils: and he cast out the spirits with *his* word, and healed all that were sick.

Now let me just give you a definition that I think will help you. The word "healed" in this passage in Matthew is the Greek word, ***therapu*** or ***therapouo***. We get our word "therapy" from it. It means "to wait upon, attend to, to relieve disease, to cure, to heal, to adore, or to worship." So because this word has so many meanings, we come to find out there is great healing therapy in praising the Lord. There is great therapy when you adore Him.

THE PRAISE CURE

When you praise His name, and thank Him in advance for your healing, you are thanking Him based on His Word. You may not feel any different and you may not look any different, but Jesus said, "By his stripes you were healed." What are you going to do? Are you going to act upon that Word? One way you can act upon it is by thanking Him, and giving Him praise. There is therapy in it.

Lillian B. Yeomans, who was a medical doctor wrote a book called, *Healing From Heaven.* There is one chapter in particular that is called "The Praise Cure." It talks about the power of praise and worship to bring a cure into your life.

She tells a story about a missionary in China who had attended to another missionary when she had smallpox. She had waited on this other missionary and served her. Then she caught the disease and broke out with pox all over her body.

And as she began to pray, the Lord said to her, "Believe that My Word is true and begin to praise me for it." Now this was back in the days where there was no cure for smallpox. But this little missionary began to praise God, to thank Him, and to give Him glory. It said in the book that she sang praises and songs she knew (and she probably made up some too). She quoted the scripture and blessed and magnified the Lord. As she got into it hour after hour, day after day, it became a lifestyle.

She just wouldn't quit, and as she praised, she was empowered. One day, as she was praising God, she had a vision where she saw a set of scales. On one scale there was a basket filled with the problem—the smallpox disease. On the other scale was a basket filled with her praises. The basket filled with the problem outweighed the basket filled with her praises. Her praise basket was only half full.

God said to her, "When your praise basket becomes full, your problem will leave." So she kept on praising God. The people thought she had lost her mind, but she just kept praising God. She praised Him all day long and it became contagious. People started praising God all around that place. She was quarantined to her room but she kept on praising God.

Then one night she had another vision. God showed her that her praise basket was full. It outweighed the problem. At that moment, the testimony said the smallpox left her body—without even leaving a scar.

A total miracle resulted from praise!

I want to know, how full is your basket of praise? It is time to get it full! Begin to praise God, and as you do, that miracle working power will go to work for you. Your praise basket will get full and it will outweigh the problem. The symptoms have to go because healing is for you! It is your gift from God.

NOTES

LESSON 11:
HEALING IS GOD'S WILL

Healing is for you and God is about to turn some things around for you. You know, you may have been sick for a very long time, but Jesus is more than enough for your situation. The Bible says that when we call upon Him, He will answer us and show us great and mighty things that we know not (Jeremiah 33:3).

In other words, He will show you things you can't even conceive or understand or be aware of. God is able to do far over and above all that we dare ask, think, hope or dream (Ephesians 3:20). What I am saying is that there is no impossible situation with God!

HEALING IS ALWAYS THE WILL OF GOD

Healing and health have always been the will of God. Scripturally, it is always God's will to heal His people and set the captives free. Now some folks have a hard time with this issue because they don't know whether it's God's will to heal them or not. And if you don't know what God's will is, then how can you believe Him for it?

So people will say things like, "Maybe God wants me sick," or "Perhaps God is trying to teach me something through this sickness," or "Maybe God put this on me for my good so I would learn how to be patient and compassionate."

Well, all of those are statements that people make, but none of them agree with scripture. In other words, God is not putting sickness and disease on His children to teach them something. You would not put disease on your children to teach them something. You train them with your words and with your example. Now you discipline your children, and God can discipline us. But He disciplines us through His Word. He brings correction through His Word.

Now if we persist in going our own way and doing our own thing by walking in willful rebellion, then we open ourselves up for trouble. This happens many times and God has nothing to do with it.

It is not God's will for you to be sick. Scripture proves that He wants us to be well and strong. I don't see in the scripture that God's plan for man ever changed. Now man changed some things and God had to respond differently, but He sent Jesus to restore man to His original intention. As a matter of fact, He gave us something better.

HEBREWS 8:6
6 But now hath he obtained a more excellent ministry, by how much also he is the mediator of a better covenant, which was established upon better promises.

If God wanted His children well in the Old Testament, how much more does He want us well in the New Testament?

GENESIS 1:1,2
1 In the beginning God created the heaven and the earth.
2 And the earth was without form, and void; and darkness was upon the face of the deep. And the Spirit of God moved upon the face of the waters.

The Spirit of God moved—and that's what's gonna' happen to many of you as you study these lessons and stay faithful to hear the Word concerning healing. The Spirit of God is going to move on you and recreate some things and make some things new and cause God's plan to come to pass.

GENESIS 1:3,4
3 And God said, Let there be light: and there was light.
4 And God saw the light, that it was good: and God divided the light from the darkness.

Now that's the little phrase that I want to point out: "God saw that it was good."

GENESIS 1:5-21
5 And God called the light Day, and the darkness he called Night. And the evening and the morning were the first day.

6 And God said, Let there be a firmament in the midst of
the waters, and let it divide the waters from the waters.
7 And God made the firmament, and divided the waters
which were under the firmament from the waters which
were above the firmament: and it was so.
8 And God called the firmament Heaven. And the
evening and the morning were the second day.
9 And God said, Let the waters under the heaven be
gathered together unto one place, and let the dry land
appear: and it was so.
10 And God called the dry land Earth; and the gathering
together of the waters called he Seas: and God saw that
it was good.
11 And God said, Let the earth bring forth grass, the herb
yielding seed, and the fruit tree yielding fruit after his
kind, whose seed is in itself, upon the earth: and it was
so.
12 And the earth brought forth grass, and herb yielding
seed after his kind, and the tree yielding fruit, whose
seed was in itself, after his kind: and God saw that it
was good.
13 And the evening and the morning were the third day.
14 And God said, Let there be lights in the firmament of
the heaven to divide the day from the night; and let
them be for signs, and for seasons, and for days, and
years:
15 And let them be for lights in the firmament of the
heaven to give light upon the earth: and it was so.
16 And God made two great lights; the greater light to rule
the day, and the lesser light to rule the night: he made
the stars also.
17 And God set them in the firmament of the heaven to
give light upon the earth,
18 And to rule over the day and over the night, and to
divide the light from the darkness: and God saw that it
was good.
19 And the evening and the morning were the fourth day.
20 And God said, Let the waters bring forth abundantly the
moving creature that hath life, and fowl that may fly
above the earth in the open firmament of heaven.
21 And God created great whales, and every living creature
that moveth, which the waters brought forth
abundantly, after their kind, and every winged fowl
after his kind: and God saw that it was good.

Here in these first few verses of Genesis, God saw what He created and said it was good, five different times in those scriptures about creation.

GENESIS 1:25-27
25 And God made the beast of the earth after his kind, and cattle after their kind, and every thing that creepeth upon the earth after his kind: and God saw that it was good.
26 And God said, Let us make man in our image, after our likeness: and let them have dominion over the fish of the sea, and over the fowl of the air, and over the cattle, and over all the earth, and over every creeping thing that creepeth upon the earth.
27 So God created man in his own image, in the image of God created he him; male and female created he them.

Did you know you are created in the image of God? You are God's highest creation.

GENESIS 1:28-31
28 And God blessed them, and God said unto them, Be fruitful, and multiply, and replenish the earth, and subdue it: and have dominion over the fish of the sea, and over the fowl of the air, and over every living thing that moveth upon the earth.
29 And God said, Behold, I have given you every herb bearing seed, which is upon the face of all the earth, and every tree, in the which is the fruit of a tree yielding seed; to you it shall be for meat.
30 And to every beast of the earth, and to every fowl of the air, and to every thing that creepeth upon the earth, wherein there is life, I have given every green herb for meat: and it was so.
31 And God saw every thing that he had made, and, behold, it was very good. And the evening and the morning were the sixth day.

All the time God said everything was good, and everything was good up till then. But when God made man in His own image, and made him to have dominion and to rule and reign and subdue the earth, He said, "It's very good!"

God made us very good. He did not make us sick. He did not make us to die from disease. God did not make us to deteriorate and to wither away. Everything He made in the beginning was good and God's plan has never changed. He is still a good God. He is still doing good things in the earth.

GOD SAW THAT IT WAS GOOD

Sickness and disease are not good. Sickness does not qualify under the heading of good. Even in the beginning, sickness had no place in God's creation. Let's look at the definition of the word "good."

PSALM 107:1

1 O give thanks unto the LORD, for he is good: for his mercy endureth for ever.

In the Hebrew concordance "good" means "beautiful, best, better, bountiful, cheerful, fair, favorable, fine, glad, gracious, joyful, kind, loving, merry, most pleasant, pleasing, pleasureful, precious, at ease, well, wealthy, sweet, ready, and prosperous." Now that's what that word "good" means. It has all those definitions under its heading and so you can see then, that sickness and disease would never qualify as a good thing.

Health and healing is beautiful. There is something beautiful about health and healing. We even use the term "better" when someone is ill. "How are they doing?" "Well, they're getting better." Anything that produces healing and health and peace and rest and joy is under the heading of good, bountiful and cheerful. When you're sick, you are not very cheerful. You are in pain. "Disease" means out of ease, or out of peace. And the very word "good" means at ease or at peace, pleasant, merry, and joyful.

God said, "It is good." In other words, "I have made my man well. I have made him beautiful. I have made my creation to abound and to be strong and merry and to be at ease." Why? "Because they are precious to me."

When God said, "It is good," He was saying all of that. "It is very beautiful. It is very bountiful. It is very pleasing and pleasant and favorable and well and strong." So God made His creation good.

It was God's will in the beginning for us to be strong and healthy and under His blessing. Sickness and disease had no place.

You say, "Well, where did it come from?" It didn't come from God. It came way back there when that old serpent, the devil got involved in the life of man. He caused Adam and Eve to disobey God and open their life up to sin. The wages of sin is death. As someone said, "disease is death begun." And when sin came in, death came in.

God created Adam to live forever. There was no disease. God created him very good. And when Satan came, he brought disease, devastation and destruction. Sickness and disease do not come from God. It was God's will in the beginning for His man to be strong and free from sickness.

As we can see, the world is not free from sickness. One third of the national budget is spent on health care alone—approximately 250 billion dollars! That doesn't include individuals that pay out of their own pockets. They are paying doctor bills, medicine bills, etc. There is enormous amounts of money being spent by Americans to stay well.

And if it is God's will for us to be sick, then why are we spending so much money to stay well? It is not God's will for us to be sick, but obviously you know that society is not free from sickness.

So God sent Jesus to redeem man from the curse of the law, which is sickness, poverty, and spiritual death (and I believe premature death), so that we could have right-standing with God restored by the blood of Jesus.

PSALM 107:19
19 Then they cry unto the LORD in their trouble, and he saveth them out of their distresses.

Do you know how much distress sickness can bring on our lives? Cry to the Lord and He will save you out of your distresses.

PSALM 107:20
20 He sent his word, and healed them, and delivered them from their destructions.

Now the word "healed" there is ***rapha.*** He sent His Word to ***rapha*** them. He sent His Word to make them strong. He sent His Word to produce goodness in our lives. He sent His Word to give us beauty, health, bountifulness, pleasure, joy and health. And to cause us to be well. He sent His Word and healed them, and delivered them from their destructions. Two thousand years ago, God laid our sins on Jesus. God laid our sickness on Jesus. God laid our death on Him and now we are alive with the life of Almighty God through faith in Jesus Christ. We can reach out with our hand of faith and our heart of love and say, "Lord, I receive my healing now."

GOD'S WILL HAS NOT CHANGED

PSALM 107:21
21 Oh that men would praise the LORD for his goodness, and for his wonderful works to the children of men!

Believe that God wants you well. Why would He create man in the beginning to be well and strong and healthy, then all of a sudden, at the end of the age, desire that you be sick?

It is not that way.

Receive your healing now. By faith reach out and say, "I believe it's mine. God wants me well. God did a very good thing when He created me. And even though Adam lost it, Jesus restored it. So I receive my healing now." Now begin to praise God for it.

Dr. Lillian B. Yeomans made this statement in her book, *Healing From Heaven,* "God created man, the head of a new order of beings, perfect in spirit, soul, and body, free from all deformity and disease, a reflection of the beauty and glories of his Creator."

ECCLESIASTES 3:14
14 I know that, whatsoever God doeth, it shall be for ever: nothing can be put to it, nor any thing taken from it: and God doeth it, that men should fear before him.

If God did something in the beginning, His purpose hasn't changed. Then Dr. Yeomans made this statement, "So this is His eternal purpose concerning us." What is the eternal purpose of

God? That you be well. That His creation be strong. You are created in His image and His likeness to be filled with the bountifulness of God's healing power. The very life, nature and energy of Jesus Christ Himself. This eternal purpose of God has never changed.

If God ever wanted you well, He wants you well today. I'm telling you sickness is an enemy and Jesus is our friend. Therefore, we can call upon Him and receive His healing power today.

ROMANS 10:17
17 So then faith cometh by hearing, and hearing by the word of God.

Receive the Word so that your faith can be built up. Faith is the hand that receives God's promises. If you'll build that faith up, you may not see a change right now, but I guarantee you the goodness of healing will be manifested in your body because healing belongs to you.

LESSON 12: OUR BENEFIT PACKAGE

3 JOHN 2
2 Beloved, I wish above all things that thou mayest prosper and be in health, even as thy soul prospereth.

The apostle John said the number one thing on his prayer list for the Church was for their prosperity and then for their health. Now when we talk about prosperity, we are not just talking about money and things to consume on ourselves. We are talking about having our needs met and being able to be abundantly supplied to meet someone else's need and to preach the gospel.

After all, God said, I will give you power to get wealth that you may establish My covenant (Deuteronomy 8:18). So God has a covenant to bless us and He wants us to be a blessing. It is important to have prosperity in order to carry the gospel to the foreign lands or to pay tithe or give to your church or to help someone in need. Health is very vital. So number one and two on John's prayer list was prosperity and health. God wants you prosperous and God wants you well. Without these you can not be at your best.

LUKE 5:15
15 But so much the more went there a fame abroad of him: and great multitudes came together to hear, and to be healed by him of their infirmities.

Do you know why many folks don't get healed? Because they don't take the time to hear any Word about healing. And if you don't hear any word about healing, you will never have faith to be healed.

God's will concerning healing has not changed. God has not changed His mind about sickness and disease. God created Adam to be well. He said when He created him that it was very good. We have already seen in the Word that "good" includes health, wellness, soundness, beauty and bountifulness.

When Jesus came, He gave us something better than what Adam had. We have a better covenant than Adam had. We have a better covenant with better promises. It can't be wiped out. It can't be reasoned away. Because Jesus sealed it once and for all, and healing belongs to us today.

PSALM 103:1
1 Bless the LORD, O my soul: and all that is within me, bless his holy name.

You know, if we just took that scripture, we would have a whole lot less trouble with sickness and disease and devils and depression and those things that try to rob us of God's best. Just bless the Lord. You say, "What do I have to bless Him about?" His love, His life, His blood. If you are saved and on your way to heaven, you can bless the Lord. You may say, "Everything is not going good in my life." I tell you, if you start blessing the Lord, things will start lining up! The Bible says, *"23 Whoso offereth praise glorifieth me: and to him that ordereth his conversation aright will I show the salvation of God."* So as you praise Him, things start coming in line and God goes to work on your behalf. Just start praising the Lord.

Be thankful that God loves you, and that He gave His son for you. Start thanking Him for that and it will change your whole world. It will turn things around for you. Proclaim God's promises for your life and He will work for you mightily. God has a plan for you and His purpose will endure forever.

Now notice He says, "Bless the Lord, O my soul," (my mind, my will, and my emotions). I have to choose to bless the Lord. "And all that is within me (my spirit, my heart) bless His holy name."

WE HAVE A BENEFIT PACKAGE

PSALM 103:2
2 Bless the LORD, O my soul, and forget not all his benefits:

You may have some benefits on your job or you may have had benefits before you retired, or at least you know what a benefit is. A benefit is something that you are better off for having. If you have health care benefits, retirement benefits, life insurance benefits, vacation benefits, or get overtime pay as a benefit, then you are better off for having them. Now it amazes me that the very thing He says for us not to forget, many Christians do forget.

PSALM 103:3-5
3 Who forgiveth all thine iniquities; who healeth all thy diseases;
4 Who redeemeth thy life from destruction; who crowneth thee with lovingkindness and tender mercies;
5 Who satisfieth thy mouth with good things; so that thy youth is renewed like the eagle's.

Here is a benefit of knowing God. He forgives all my iniquities! That is a benefit. If you have sinned, why don't you run to God and ask Him to forgive you? You might be a backslidden minister of the gospel thinking God doesn't want you any more, "How can God receive me back and forgive me of what I have done?" I'm telling you, it is one of your benefits. And you can run to Him and say "God, forgive me. I receive my benefit."

Wouldn't it seem silly to work for an employer and give your time and energy to them, work for years and when the time came to take your vacation, you just backed off and said, "Well, I know it's my benefit, but I just don't feel I'm worthy to take that benefit." The employer would wonder what kind of employee he had. That benefit belongs to you.

Don't shrink back from the benefits God gives you.

- **Benefit #1:** *He forgives all your iniquities.* Did you see the word "all"? Don't let the devil hold anything over your head.

- **Benefit #2:** *He heals all your diseases.* If "all" means anything, it means everything. And He says He heals **all** your diseases. So that qualifies you for healing right there. That means AIDS, cancer, allergies—everything. All means all!

- **Benefit #3:** *He redeems your life from destruction.* Have you had any destruction or misery lately? I want you to know that God redeems or buys you back or rescues you or pulls you out of destruction.

How is He going to do it? I don't know. He is the Almighty God. He is the one that offers the benefits, we just accept them. Let me tell you something. God will never go bankrupt and you will never have to forfeit your benefits either. He will always be able to carry them out.

- **Benefit #4:** *He crowns you with loving kindness and tender mercies.* You know, some folks think that God is up there waiting for them to make a mistake so that He can knock them in the head or crown them with something besides loving kindness and tender mercies! Part of your benefit package is to have God's crown, God's anointing, God's blessing of love and mercy in your life. He wants you to treat others with loving kindness and tender mercies also.

- **Benefit #5:** *He satisfies your mouth with good things so that your youth is renewed like the eagle's.* A good God satisfies us with good. The word "things" is italicized in my Bible. That means it wasn't in the original manuscripts. The translators put it there to clarify the meaning. But I like to say, "He satisfies my mouth with good." Remember that good means "bountiful, beautiful, the best, favorable, fine, joyful, well, wealth, sweet, prosperous, health and strength.

Now those are your benefits. Don't forget them!

The first benefit is "He forgives all your iniquities." Now there is probably no one that knows anything about God or Christianity that would deny that benefit. Well, if one benefit is that sure, then why wouldn't the other ones be? The same God who gave you the first benefit gave you the other four.

LUKE 7:36-50
36 And one of the Pharisees desired him that he would eat with him. And he went into the Pharisee's house, and sat down to meat.
37 And, behold, a woman in the city, which was a sinner, when she knew that Jesus sat at meat in the Pharisee's house, brought an alabaster box of ointment,
38 And stood at his feet behind him weeping, and began to wash his feet with tears, and did wipe them with the hairs of her head, and kissed his feet, and anointed them with the ointment.

39 Now when the Pharisee which had bidden him saw it, he spake within himself, saying, This man, if he were a prophet, would have known who and what manner of woman this is that toucheth him: for she is a sinner.
40 And Jesus answering said unto him, Simon, I have somewhat to say unto thee. And he saith, Master, say on.
41 There was a certain creditor which had two debtors: the one owed five hundred pence, and the other fifty.
42 And when they had nothing to pay, he frankly forgave them both. Tell me therefore, which of them will love him most?
43 Simon answered and said, I suppose that he, to whom he forgave most. And he said unto him, Thou hast rightly judged.
44 And he turned to the woman, and said unto Simon, Seest thou this woman? I entered into thine house, thou gavest me no water for my feet: but she hath washed my feet with tears, and wiped them with the hairs of her head.
45 Thou gavest me no kiss: but this woman since the time I came in hath not ceased to kiss my feet.
46 My head with oil thou didst not anoint: but this woman hath anointed my feet with ointment.
47 Wherefore I say unto thee, Her sins, which are many, are forgiven; for she loved much: but to whom little is forgiven, the same loveth little.
48 And he said unto her, Thy sins are forgiven.
49 And they that sat at meat with him began to say within themselves, Who is this that forgiveth sins also?
50 And he said to the woman, Thy faith hath saved thee; go in peace.

Now in the eyes of those Pharisees, those religious leaders, this woman couldn't be forgiven. But David wrote back there in Psalm 103:3, *"Who forgiveth all thine iniquities…"* There is not a sin that He can not or will not or has not forgiven. There is not a person that His blood can not cleanse. There is not a heart that He can't change. If that is true for the forgiveness of sin, then it is true concerning sickness and disease.

Jesus said unto that woman, *"Thy sins are forgiven."* He is saying that to you and me today. Forgiveness belongs to us. They were criticizing Him and Jesus looked at her and said, *"Thy faith hath saved thee; go in peace."*

THE FAITH THAT SAVES IS THE FAITH THAT HEALS

Now here is another point I want to make. God wants your life to be peaceful. There are a lot of situations that come at us to rob our peace: sin, failure, shortcomings, trials, tribulations, sickness and disease. All of these try to rob us of our peace. God wants your life to be peaceful.

If you haven't accepted Jesus today, you don't have any peace. Your sins may be many, but you can be forgiven today. And if you are sick, your sickness may be great, but you can be healed today! The same God that gave His Son to save you, gave His Son to heal you. You've got a great benefit package. It belongs to you.

Remember, the faith that saves you is the same faith that heals you. The word "saved" is the Greek word ***sozo.*** It means preservation, safety, to be healed, delivered, prospered or made whole. If our faith saved us, why can't our faith heal us? There are two reasons why our faith couldn't heal us: #1, if God had never provided healing for us in the first place; and #2, if we never released our faith.

Well God did provide healing for us. If this woman's faith in Luke 7 could save her from a life of sin, then your faith can save you from a life of sickness. Now what I want you to do is say, "I believe healing is mine. It is one of my benefits." Praise God for it and expect Him to perform it in your life. Thank God healing is the children's bread and it belongs to you!

LESSON 13: RELEASE YOUR FAITH BY SAYING

Faith comes by hearing and hearing by the Word of God. Do you understand that if faith can save you, faith can heal you? Faith can deliver us. When I say faith, I mean confidence and trust in God and His promises. Faith is so strong that it motivates us to action. Faith without action is dead.

PSALM 103:1-5

1 **A Psalm of David. Bless the LORD, O my soul: and all that is within me, bless his holy name.**

2 **Bless the LORD, O my soul, and forget not all his benefits:**

3 **Who forgiveth all thine iniquities; who healeth all thy diseases;**

4 **Who redeemeth thy life from destruction; who crowneth thee with lovingkindness and tender mercies;**

5 **Who satisfieth thy mouth with good things; so that thy youth is renewed like the eagle's.**

Right at the top of the benefits list, God mentions forgiveness of sin and healing for our bodies. Thank God these are benefits that Jesus paid for so that we can enjoy them.

Remember in our last lesson we looked in Luke 7 at the story of a woman who was a great sinner. She came to Jesus and anointed and washed His feet with her tears and dried them with her hair. The religious Pharisee got upset. Jesus said this woman has done something wonderful. She has displayed an attitude of heart repentance toward me. And then, in verse 47, He said that her sins which had been many were forgiven. He looked at this woman and said, *"Thy faith hath saved thee; go in peace,"* (verse 50).

GOD IS THE AUTHOR OF LIFE

God wants peace in your life. Sickness and disease do not bring peace. They bring pain. God is not the author of pain, disease and death. He is the author of life, revelation, wisdom and peace. He is a healing God and healing belongs to us.

Now in Mark 5, there was a woman who needed healing.

MARK 5:25-34
25 And a certain woman, which had an issue of blood twelve years,
26 And had suffered many things of many physicians, and had spent all that she had, and was nothing bettered, but rather grew worse,
27 When she had heard of Jesus, came in the press behind, and touched his garment.
28 For she said, If I may touch but his clothes, I shall be whole.
29 And straightway the fountain of her blood was dried up; and she felt in her body that she was healed of that plague.
30 And Jesus, immediately knowing in himself that virtue had gone out of him, turned him about in the press, and said, Who touched my clothes?
31 And his disciples said unto him, Thou seest the multitude thronging thee, and sayest thou, Who touched me?
32 And he looked round about to see her that had done this thing.
33 But the woman fearing and trembling, knowing what was done in her, came and fell down before him, and told him all the truth.
34 And he said unto her, Daughter, thy faith hath made thee whole; go in peace, and be whole of thy plague.

She said in verse 28, *"If I may touch but his clothes, I shall be whole."* If you are born again, you have faith because you couldn't get saved without it. *"For by grace are ye saved through faith..."* (Ephesians 2:8). So the Word gave you faith to be saved. Therefore, you have faith now, but you need to grow and develop it, and it has to be released.

This woman said, *"If I may touch but his clothes, I shall be whole."* That was her faith talking. **And she released her faith by saying.** In other words, if faith is in your spirit, then how are you going to release it? Well, you have to open your mouth and say what you believe.

FAITH SPEAKS

2 CORINTHIANS 4:13
13 We having the same spirit of faith, according as it is written, I believed, and therefore have I spoken; we also believe, and therefore speak;

Faith is not completed just because it resides in your spirit or just because you believe something. That is the beginning of faith—you hear the Word and faith comes into your heart. With the heart man believes (Romans 10:10), but it doesn't stop there. Notice this scripture says I believe therefore I speak. That is when faith is released. When you believe something you will say it.

This little woman in Mark 5 believed what she heard about Jesus would benefit her life. She must have heard that Jesus was a healer. She must have heard that some folks were getting set free from diseases, infirmities and weaknesses. She must have heard that the sick were being healed because she showed up with her sickness and she intended to get through that crowd and touch His garment.

How do we know that? Because she said, *"If I may touch but his clothes, I shall be whole."* Now that was her faith talking. And that faith was in her heart. First she heard it, second, she believed it, and third, she did it. She acted on her faith and she received her miracle. Verse 29 said, *"And straightway the fountain of her blood was dried up; and she felt in her body that she was healed of that plague."*

Many of you haven't felt good for a long time. But I want you to know that Jesus wants you to feel good. Now faith and feeling many times don't agree. We are to walk by faith and not by sight, not by feelings, not in the natural realm, (2 Corinthians 5:7). We are to walk by faith in God's promises.

But it says here that she "felt in her body." God will produce good feelings and health in you. Health is feeling good. Health belongs to you. She felt in her body that she was healed of the plague. Something took place in her right there. A miracle happened at that very moment. She could tell that the fountain or flow or hemorrhage of blood was dried up.

She quit bleeding. She was strengthened. I believe she stood up when she felt she was healed. And Jesus, in verse 30, *"knowing in himself that virtue had gone out of him, turned him about in the press, and said, Who touched my clothes?"* He knew somebody had touched Him with the touch of faith. This woman reached out on purpose and touched Him by faith. And she received her miracle.

THE CYCLE OF FAITH

When you think of a cycle of faith, that one is a good cycle. **Hear it, believe it in your heart, say it, do it, receive it, tell it.** Boy, she testified, she told the whole truth. She said, "I've been sick for 12 years and I've spent everything I had, but I got worse and worse. Then I heard of Jesus. I believed that if I could get to this meeting, then I would be healed. So I reached out and I said what I believed. I reached out and touched Him and I received my miracle. Now, I'm telling everyone that I've been healed."

Then, notice what Jesus said to her, *"Daughter, thy faith hath made thee whole; go in peace, and be whole of thy plague,"* (verse 34).

Now in Luke 7, Jesus said something similar to the woman who came and washed His feet. He told her that she had been forgiven of her sins. He said, *"Thy faith hath saved thee; go in peace,"* (verse 50).

Did you notice that little phrase in both of these examples? "Go in peace." God wants us to be in peace. Do you know what "peace" means? It means "freedom from fear, freedom from agitating passions and moral and physical conflict." And I think we could add freedom from financial conflict.

"Go in peace." They could go in peace because their faith had been demonstrated. Their faith had been released and God had answered their prayers. Jesus said it was their faith that saved or healed them.

You know many times we want to get healed on someone else's faith. You may not be able to get to a great healing meeting or prayer service or anointed evangelist. But you can touch Jesus right where you are at. Your faith can reach through the crowd of doubt, despair, discouragement, pain and disease and touch Him.

The healing power of God is available. Believe that it is yours and receive it and thank Him for it. He will work a miracle for you. Then you will be able to go in peace. You could rise up off of that bed of sickness or out of that depression and go in peace, freedom, provision, and power.

As you begin to praise His name in faith, believing that healing belongs to you, then God will cause His Spirit to bring the delivering manifestation. Healing is yours and it does belong to you because of what Jesus has done. Receive your benefit package and thank God for it. You will see results!

NOTES

LESSON 14:

JESUS IS THE GOOD SHEPHERD

Healing is the children's bread. God will heal you today to show you that He loves you if you will dare believe Him. Healing is in the package deal. If you've never been saved, let His love and healing power flow into your life and let Him prove Himself strong on your behalf. The Bible calls Jesus a compassionate high priest and He has got great plans for your life.

JESUS CAME TO GIVE US LIFE

JOHN 10:10
10 **The thief cometh not, but for to steal, and to kill, and to destroy: I am come that they might have life, and that they might have it more abundantly.**

The thief that Jesus is talking about is the devil. He tries to rob you. He tries to rob you of your health, you finances, your children, and anything that produces peace and joy and blessing.

Jesus went on to say, *"I am come that they might have life, and that they might have it more abundantly."* Now that scripture alone would tell you that healing is for you today. If Jesus came to produce or give us abundant life, then obviously healing is included in that life. Sickness is in death's package deal and healing is in life's package deal.

Healing keeps you living. Sickness will cause you to die or deteriorate, wear out, and be ineffective. Healing will produce health, strength, and effectiveness in your life. I think we could put in that scripture, "I have come that they might have life or that they might be well or that they might have healing and health more abundantly." I don't think this would be a misinterpretation of the purpose and intention of God in the plan of redemption.

THE GOOD SHEPHERD

Now notice what Jesus says in verse 11.

JOHN 10:11
11 I am the good shepherd: the good shepherd giveth his life for the sheep.

If Jesus is the good shepherd, then our good shepherd is not making us sick. Our good shepherd is the one that is making us well. His desire is for us to move on into His best.

A good shepherd is the shepherd that tends the sheep. A good shepherd is a shepherd that helps the sheep. A good shepherd is a shepherd that protects the sheep or brings healing to the sheep.

We read in Psalm 23 about the Lord being our shepherd. This is a psalm for living. It is where we are today. The 22nd Psalm is what Jesus quoted on the cross, the 23rd Psalm is what we have today because of the death, burial and resurrection, and the 24th Psalm is the King of Glory returning for His own!

PSALM 23
1 A Psalm of David. The LORD is my shepherd; I shall not want.
2 He maketh me to lie down in green pastures: he leadeth me beside the still waters.
3 He restoreth my soul: he leadeth me in the paths of righteousness for his name's sake.
4 Yea, though I walk through the valley of the shadow of death, I will fear no evil: for thou art with me; thy rod and thy staff they comfort me.
5 Thou preparest a table before me in the presence of mine enemies: thou anointest my head with oil; my cup runneth over.
6 Surely goodness and mercy shall follow me all the days of my life: and I will dwell in the house of the LORD for ever.

Aren't you glad you're walking through the valley and not camping out it in? There is an end to your problem. There is an end to your trial. There is an end to that sickness and disease that has come at your body.

God is preparing a table of healing for you today in the presence of your infirmity. Right in the midst of that sickness and disease, God's got you a table of divine healing and health. Would you dare partake of His table today by faith?

He said, "I prepare a table before you in the presence of your enemies." So right in the midst of the storm is where the table is. The devil says, "You're not going to get well, you are going to die. There's no hope and there's no future. Look for a table that God prepares right in the midst of that problem.

The Bible says "in the presence of your enemy." Sickness is an enemy because it steals, kills and destroys. It is a thief because it robs you of your health, your well being, your peace, your joy and everything that is good.

Remember that healing is one of God's goodnesses. Verse 6 says, *"Surely goodness and mercy shall follow me all the days of my life: and I will dwell in the house of the LORD for ever."*

THE OIL OF HEALING

One thing that I wanted to point out in this scripture is that there is healing, health, provision, peace, restoration, joy, and victory all through that psalm. But he said in verse 5, He *"anointest my head with oil..."*

The good shepherd was over the sheep. In the beginning of the day, he would anoint their heads with oil. Why? Because those sheep stood there grazing throughout the day with their heads down. They would bump into rocks and twigs and other things that would cut their heads. And that oil would already be there to just drip right down into the wound to bring healing, health and protection.

Jesus cares so much about you that He has provided the oil and the ointment of healing before sickness comes. So you know that He is concerned for you when you are in the midst of that problem and you are devastated by that disease.

When you can't seem to get the victory over that pressure, pain or problem, He will come to your rescue speedily. He will heal you and set you free. He will work in you mightily if you will dare to believe it.

If the good shepherd cared enough about the sheep to give them some "pre" medicine and some "pre" cure and some "pre" health, I want you to know that Jesus will come running to mend that wounded heart, or broken leg, or wounded spirit.

There are people whose physical bodies are okay and they don't seem to have any disease showing on the outside or any infirmity that would be classified as physical. But they've got a broken spirit. They are wounded and are hurting—they have been emotionally damaged. Jesus came to set every captive free!

LUKE 4:18

18 The Spirit of the Lord is upon me, because he hath anointed me to preach the gospel to the poor; he hath sent me to heal the brokenhearted, to preach deliverance to the captives, and recovering of sight to the blind, to set at liberty them that are bruised,

Right there the second thing Jesus said God had anointed Him to do was to heal the brokenhearted. Then He said God sent Him to preach deliverance to the captives.

Some of you may not be sick in your body with a disease, but you are bound by drugs, alcohol, nicotine and perversion. I want you to know those are sicknesses in themselves. Those are bondages in themselves. This same message will set you free because He is a healing, delivering, powerful, good Jesus. And He came to preach deliverance.

He said, "I came to preach recovery of sight to the blind." If you need a miracle, He'll give you one. He said, "I came to set at liberty them that are bruised." The Amplified Bible says, "broken down by calamity." You know sometimes you can only take so much. You can stand strong through the storms, but storm after storm, it seems like it breaks you down. I tell you, Jesus comes to lift you up today because He's a healing Jesus. He has come to heal your broken heart and to deliver you from drugs, alcohol and perversion. He has come to heal your body and to give you a miracle.

Why not let Him? Why not reach out to Him and say, "Jesus, I believe You're my shepherd and I receive your healing power now." It is available to you if you'll believe it and receive it.

I don't know what you've been through, and maybe nobody on earth knows what you've been through, but Jesus does. Jesus knows exactly what you've been through and He is the one that can heal and make you whole again.

You remember there in Luke 4 where He stood up to read in the synagogue? This was the first recorded message after He was set apart to go into His ministry. He read that scripture, "I've been anointed to preach deliverance to the captives and the gospel to the poor and to heal the brokenhearted."

It is time for you to be healed. It is time for you to release your faith in Jesus Christ and His bountiful love and accept His healing power. If you've been bound by anything, He will set you free. God's big enough to handle your problem. Reach out by faith and say, "He heals, He delivers, and He sets the captive free!" Start praising Him for it.

You may have parts of your body that are missing. You know, God is a miracle worker and your faith in Him can make you whole. Let the healing power of God flow into your life. Let the miracle working power of God come from heaven to you. Start believing things can change. God has spare parts and He'll give you some if you'll believe Him.

The power of the good shepherd is available right now for your life. So, take that care and put it on God!

NOTES

LESSON 15: HE IS FULL OF COMPASSION

Healing is for you according to God's Word. Not only did God lay our sins on Jesus, but He laid our sicknesses and diseases on Him too. Isaiah said in his report, "Surely he has borne our sicknesses and carried our diseases," (Isaiah 53:4). Thank God for the healing power that comes through faith in Jesus.

Praise God, we've got a high priest and His name is Jesus. The Bible says He is the high priest of our confession. In other words, what we declare to be true according to the Word with our faith, He will see to it, or He will watch over it to make it good.

HOLD FAST YOUR PROFESSION

HEBREWS 4:14
14 Seeing then that we have a great high priest, that is passed into the heavens, Jesus the Son of God, let us hold fast our profession [or confession]**.**

You remember in Mark 5, the little woman that had the issue of blood for twelve years? She was sick, she had spent all that she had and was nothing better, but just got worse and worse. When she heard about Jesus, faith came because faith comes by hearing and hearing by the Word of God.

She heard He was healing people around the country and she believed that He would heal her. The Bible says that she started *saying.* Now who did she say it to? I don't know. She might have said it to her neighbors, her husband, or herself. She said, "If I can just get over there and touch His garment, I shall be made whole." That was her profession. That was her confession. That was her faith talking.

The Bible says that we have a high priest that is listening to our profession. It implies that in the scripture. We have a high priest and He has passed into the heavens. So let us hold fast our profession.

Did you know that your faith touches God? Your faith is what reaches God. And your faith is not only something that's in your heart, but it is something that is released with your words or your mouth and your actions. The little woman believed it, she said it, and then she did it. She actually pressed through that crowd and touched His garment and she received her healing! Then she told it, and kept telling it. I believe she told everybody, "I told you if I went over there and touched His garment I'd be healed!"

That is a real cycle of faith: hear it, say it, do it, receive it and tell it. Jesus is listening to your profession, so hold fast to it.

THE CONFESSION OF OUR FAITH

You do have a confession today and you are saying something. It is just a matter of what you are saying. What are you professing? Are you professing what God says, or just what the doctor says? So whatever your profession is—what you say is what you're going to have.

HEBREWS 4:15
15 For we have not an high priest which cannot be touched with the feeling of our infirmities; but was in all points tempted like as we are, yet without sin.

We have a high priest that can be touched with our feelings. He knows what we are going through. He was tempted in all points yet without sin.

HEBREWS 4:16
16 Let us therefore come boldly unto the throne of grace, that we may obtain mercy, and find grace to help in time of need.

I believe that one of the ways that we come boldly to the throne of grace is with our confession or with our faith. One of the things that makes faith so easy is to realize who we have faith in and what His attitude toward us is. I can have faith in somebody that I know loves me. I can have faith in somebody that I believe cares for me. I can have faith in somebody that I believe would never hurt me. It is easy to have faith in a compassionate God. But many people don't know that God is full of compassion.

UNDERSTANDING THE LORD'S COMPASSION

PSALM 145:8
8 The LORD is gracious, and full of compassion; slow to anger, and of great mercy.

The picture that some people paint even in pulpits, is not the right picture. Sometimes the picture that some people see in their lives is not a picture of a Lord that is gracious and full of compassion, and that is slow to anger and of great mercy. **He is full of compassion.** The Lord we are talking about today is a compassionate Lord.

Understanding the Lord's compassion will help your faith for healing. The word "compassion" in the New Testament could be translated "mercy." Mercy and compassion are translated from the same word. And you will find that true in the Old Testament in many cases. When you think about God's mercy, you think about God's compassion.

The book of Hebrews says, "Let us come boldly to the throne of grace so we may obtain mercy—or obtain compassion—and find grace to help in the time of need." Anything God does for humanity is a manifestation of His mercy or His compassion.

God wants us to have faith in His mercy. We have faith in His mercy to forgive our sins. Why can't we have faith in His mercy to heal our diseases? They are in the same benefit package. It is God's mercy and compassion that causes that to come to pass.

One definition of mercy and compassion is this: "a yearning or an inner desire to help." That's why it says, "Come boldly to...obtain mercy and find grace to help in time of need." So mercy is helpful, and compassion is helpful.

Healing belongs to you and God's compassion will bring it to you if you'll have faith in it.

MATTHEW 9:34,35
34 **But the Pharisees said, He casteth out devils through the prince of the devils.**
35 **And Jesus went about all the cities and villages, teaching in their synagogues, and preaching the gospel of the kingdom, and healing every sickness and every disease among the people.**

Well, that settles it there. Your sickness or disease qualifies for healing. Because He healed every kind—and that includes the one that's on your body or in your life.

MATTHEW 9:36
36 **But when he saw the multitudes, he was moved with compassion on them, because they fainted, and were scattered abroad, as sheep having no shepherd.**

Now that scripture plainly tells us that when He saw the multitudes that were scattered, He was moved with compassion. It was compassion that moved Him to Calvary. It was compassion that moved Him to save the lost. And it is still compassion that moves Him to save the lost today.

God's compassion is involved in the forgiveness of sins. Another definition of "compassion" is "willingness to help." God is willing to forgive sins. I don't care what you've done, where you've been or what's happened in your life. He is willing to forgive you. God has the ability and the willingness—He is eager—to show Himself strong on your behalf.

You can take an old sinner that's just lost and living in the bottom of the barrel of sin, but the moment he looks to God, God is able, willing and eager to forgive him. Why? Because He is full of compassion.

MATTHEW 15:29-31
29 **And Jesus departed from thence, and came nigh unto the sea of Galilee; and went up into a mountain, and sat down there.**
30 **And great multitudes came unto him, having with them those that were lame, blind, dumb, maimed, and many others, and cast them down at Jesus' feet; and he healed them:**

31 Insomuch that the multitude wondered, when they saw the dumb to speak, the maimed to be whole, the lame to walk, and the blind to see: and they glorified the God of Israel.

We are still glorifying Him because He is still a healing Jesus, and He's got healing available for you. It belongs to you. Notice there's a great multitude—a lot of sick folk and a lot of people there.

MATTHEW 15:32-38

32 Then Jesus called his disciples unto him, and said, I have compassion on the multitude, because they continue with me now three days, and have nothing to eat: and I will not send them away fasting, lest they faint in the way.

33 And his disciples say unto him, Whence should we have so much bread in the wilderness, as to fill so great a multitude?

34 And Jesus saith unto them, How many loaves have ye? And they said, Seven, and a few little fishes.

35 And he commanded the multitude to sit down on the ground.

36 And he took the seven loaves and the fishes, and gave thanks, and brake them, and gave to his disciples, and the disciples to the multitude.

37 And they did all eat, and were filled: and they took up of the broken meat that was left seven baskets full.

38 And they that did eat were four thousand men, beside women and children.

Now you know there was somewhere in the neighborhood of eight to ten thousand people in that multitude and they all ate from seven loaves and a few fish. That is a miracle. It came to pass because of His compassion, His willingness to help them. He was not only able, but He was willing and eager.

The same compassion that moved Him to the lost, moved Him to these that were hungry and needed a miracle. Now do you think He has less compassion on the man that's on the street and has no food, shelter, or clothing, than He has on the man that's lost and filled with sin and on his way to hell? The same compassionate high priest is releasing His compassion for the lost and for the lonely and for the hurting people. That compassion that gives the miracle of the loaves and the fishes will also give the miracle of the new birth. Compassion is involved in saving souls and working miracles.

MATTHEW 14:13,14
13 When Jesus heard of it, he departed thence by ship into a desert place apart: and when the people had heard thereof, they followed him on foot out of the cities.
14 And Jesus went forth, and saw a great multitude, and was moved with compassion toward them, and he healed their sick.

He was moved with compassion to save the lost. He was moved with compassion to work miracles even to feed their hungry bellies. And He was moved with compassion to heal their bodies.

The same compassionate Jesus is no less compassionate today. He has compassion toward you, and if you're sick in your body, if you're homeless or hungry, His compassion is available to move Him to supply your need.

Do you need a financial miracle? He'll have compassion on you. Are you lost? He'll have compassion on you. He has a yearning, eager desire to bless you! Can't you have faith in someone like that? Can't you have faith in a compassionate Lord that has already said, "I'm willing, I'm able, I'm eager?"

Just believe in His compassion and you will receive your miracle. It is available to you and He is a compassionate high priest.

F.F. Bosworth has a chapter in his powerful book, *Christ the Healer,* called "The Lord's Compassion." He made a statement in there that he saw more people healed when he ministered on the Lord's compassion than anything else.

God is willing to heal you. Remember the leper that came to Jesus? He said, "If you will, you can make me whole." Jesus didn't hesitate, He said, "I am willing. Be made whole." **Have faith in God's willingness, not just in His ability.** Faith in God's ability alone is not enough to produce that miracle. It is faith in His willingness.

His attitude toward you is a loving, willing, healing attitude. He is able. He is willing. And He is eager.

NOTES

LESSON 16: DOCTOR JESUS

PSALM 107:20
20 He sent his word, and healed them, and delivered them from their destructions.

God sent His Word and healed them. The word "healed" there is ***rapha*** as in Exodus 15:26, "*...for I am the LORD that healeth thee*" or "...for I am ***Jehovah Rapha.***" So, the Lord that heals us sent His Word that we might be healed. There is healing in the Word. **God's Word is healing.**

PROVERBS 4:20-22
20 My son, attend to my words; incline thine ear unto my sayings.
21 Let them not depart from thine eyes; keep them in the midst of thine heart.
22 For they are life unto those that find them, and health to all their flesh.

These verses tell us that we are responsible to do some things concerning the Word of God. If we will incline our ears to His sayings, keep them before our eyes and in the midst of our hearts, then they will be life to us and health to all our flesh.

God's Word is medicine. The word "health" means "medicine" in the Hebrew. God's Word is medicine to all our flesh. I heard somebody call it the "gos-pill." The Word will produce healing in you. It will produce life in you. It will produce victory in your life. But you have to attend to it. You've got to hear it, keep it before you eyes, and in the midst of your heart.

THE FIRST PATIENT

MATTHEW 8:1,2
1 When he was come down from the mountain, great multitudes followed him.
2 And, behold, there came a leper and worshipped him, saying, Lord, if thou wilt, thou canst make me clean.

Dr. Lillian B. Yeomans has a book entitled, *Healing From Heaven.* In one of the chapters, she refers to this passage of scripture. She calls this leper here Jesus' first patient. Jesus is going to have two or three other patients in this chapter, then finally He'll have a whole mountainside full of patients.

So, this first patient comes to Dr. Jesus and says, "If you will, you can make me clean." He said, "I believe you have the power, I'm just concerned whether you are willing to do it for me or not." You know, a lot of Christians are like that today.

How can we ever doubt the willingness of God concerning healing when it's all through the Word? **Jesus was God's will manifested in the flesh** and the Bible said everywhere He went He did good and healed the sick. So we can see that if Jesus is the will of God, and if He went about doing good and healing, then it must have been God's will to heal people. On the other hand, how would you like your children to accuse you having the ability to help them, but not being willing to?

THE LORD'S WILLINGNESS

When we look at the cross of Calvary, I believe God's willingness is displayed. And it's written in red—the blood of His Son. That was the ultimate test of willingness. God is willing for you to be healed. The very word "compassion" means "willingness to heal, help, bring aid and deliverance."

We would never doubt God's willingness to save the sinner, so we should never doubt His willingness to heal the sick. The same God that saved us from our sins, is the same God that laid our sickness and disease upon His Son.

MATTHEW 8:2-4

2 And, behold, there came a leper and worshipped him, saying, Lord, if thou wilt, thou canst make me clean.

3 And Jesus put forth his hand, and touched him, saying, I will; be thou clean. And immediately his leprosy was cleansed.

4 And Jesus saith unto him, See thou tell no man; but go thy way, show thyself to the priest, and offer the gift that Moses commanded, for a testimony unto them.

The Lord displayed His willingness right there in verse 3. Not only is God able to heal, but He is willing.

In verse 4, Jesus was not telling people not to testify about the good things He had done for them, because you will find in the Bible that people told everything God did for them. But He was saying, "Go show the man that has the authority to pronounce you clean." Under the law, the priest was the one that had the authority to pronounce the leper clean.

God's miracle-working power will stand up under the investigation of the doctors. Thank God for doctors. But thank God for the healing power that comes from heaven. God's healing power will work a miracle in you, and when you go back to the doctor, the very thing he thought he saw on the x-ray, he won't be able to find! Because God's miracle working power will stand up under the investigation of the doctor. They have authority in the natural realm to pronounce you well. But God has already pronounced you clean, healed and delivered by faith in Jesus Christ!

Stand on the Word of God to provide the cure. Take medicine to relieve the symptom, but stand on the Word of God to provide the cure. God's willingness to heal is apparent throughout His Word.

THE SECOND PATIENT

MATTHEW 8:5-7

5 **And when Jesus was entered into Capernaum, there came unto him a centurion, beseeching him,**

6 **And saying, Lord, my servant lieth at home sick of the palsy, grievously tormented.**

7 **And Jesus saith unto him, I will come and heal him.**

Now, there's another "I will come and heal him." It had to be God's will for this man to be well. "I will come." He is coming to you through His Word. He is wanting you to know that His willingness is available to you today. So receive it. He has already come and healed you by the death, burial and resurrection of Jesus. You just need to exercise your faith in His healing power.

MATTHEW 8:8-10

8 **The centurion answered and said, Lord, I am not worthy that thou shouldest come under my roof: but speak the word only, and my servant shall be healed.**

9 **For I am a man under authority, having soldiers under me: and I say to this man, Go, and he goeth; and to another, Come, and he cometh; and to my servant, Do this, and he doeth it.**

10 **When Jesus heard it, he marvelled, and said to them that followed, Verily I say unto you, I have not found so great faith, no, not in Israel.**

Jesus marveled at this man's faith. The centurion said, "Just speak the word, and my servant will be healed. This man believed in the authority of the word of Jesus Christ.

When it comes to faith, we must accept the authority of God's Word. We take the authority of God's Word and realize that when spoken, it carries power and dominion. That spoken Word is our access into God's blessings. We can speak the Word of God into any situation we are facing. One translation of Jeremiah 1:12 says, "I watch over my Word to perform it."

ISAIAH 55:10-11

10 **For as the rain cometh down, and the snow from heaven, and returneth not thither, but watereth the earth, and maketh it bring forth and bud, that it may give seed to the sower, and bread to the eater:**

11 **So shall my word be that goeth forth out of my mouth: it shall not return unto me void, but it shall accomplish that which I please, and it shall prosper in the thing whereto I sent it.**

When you speak the Word of God, you are releasing that word in the earth. God is watching over that word to perform it and cause it to accomplish the very thing He sent it forth to accomplish.

When you find scriptures in the Bible that are impregnated with healing and health and strength, and you begin to take them as your own, and speak them out of your mouth, you are releasing that word toward God and He watches over it to perform it. We are not performing the word, He is. But we are the ones believing the word and we are the ones speaking the word, and trusting in the authority of God's holy Word.

When Jesus heard this centurion in Matthew 8, He said, "I've not seen so great a faith in all Israel." This man understood the authority. He said, "Lord, you just say it. You just speak it and my servant will be healed."

Do you realize that two thousand years ago the courts of heaven spoke out your healing with authority? Isaiah 53:4 says, "Surely He has borne our diseases and carried our pains." He did it! So the Word of God has been released. If we'll speak that Word, receive that Word, and release that Word, then He'll perform it. Begin to say, "By His stripes I am healed. I receive the healing miracle power of God into my life. He has the power and He is willing. I speak forth that promise and God watches over that word to perform it."

THE THIRD PATIENT

MATTHEW 8:14,15

14 And when Jesus was come into Peter's house, he saw his wife's mother laid, and sick of a fever.

15 And he touched her hand, and the fever left her: and she arose, and ministered unto them.

Here Jesus has come into a family situation. Peter's mother-in-law is sick, and Jesus reaches out His hand, touches her, and sets her free. Immediately, she rises up full of God's healing power and begins to serve them. Isn't that wonderful? God sets us free for service. God heals us so that we can be of service to the kingdom of God and so that we can help humanity.

MANY PATIENTS

MATTHEW 8:16

16 When the even was come, they brought unto him many that were possessed with devils: and he cast out the spirits with his word, and healed all that were sick:

He healed all that were sick. So, your sickness would qualify. He healed all sickness and disease. He cast out devils. Some of the people had evil spirits in their bodies. Others were just under the influence of that infirmity or that disease. Jesus spoke the word and set them free and healed all that were sick.

This Jesus is the same yesterday, today and forever! (Hebrews 13:8) If He healed the sick then, He's healing the sick today and you are a candidate for healing! If you are sick or bound by infirmity or disease, then Jesus is your healer. He wants you well. Healing belongs to you. It is for you.

Believe that promise. Believe He's willing. Believe He's got the power. Begin to agree with God's Word. Begin to agree with verse 17:

MATTHEW 8:17
17 **That it might be fulfilled which was spoken by Esaias the prophet, saying, Himself took our infirmities, and bareour sicknesses.**

There is nothing like the Word to fill you with faith, hope and purpose. I encourage you to avail yourself to it. Faith comes by hearing and hearing by the Word of God. And when you find that rich promise that goes off in your spirit, claim it as your own. Meditate on it. Let it take spiritual root in your heart and it will produce fruit in your body.

Reach out and grab hold of your healing by faith today. Boldly say, "Healing belongs to me!" God will perform it in your life and you will rise up strong and healthy in the power of His name!

LESSON 17:
REDEEMED FROM THE CURSE

GALATIANS 3:13
13 Christ hath redeemed us from the curse of the law, being made a curse for us: for it is written, Cursed is every one that hangeth on a tree:

Dr. Lillian B. Yeomans writes about a woman that she was ministering to who, at that time had tuberculosis. Now, tuberculosis was a deadly disease in those days and there was no cure for it. Dr. Yeomans would go in and read healing scriptures to this woman. But she focused mainly on the third chapter of Galatians and the twenty-eighth chapter of Deuteronomy.

Galatians 3 talks about the blessing of Abraham coming upon the gentiles because Christ has redeemed us from the curse of the law. And Deuteronomy 28, of course, is the listing of the blessings and the curses of the law.

So Dr. Yeomans read these two chapters over and over to this woman. She was getting the Word inside of her. She told her, "You know over here in Deuteronomy 28, verse 22, the Bible said that consumption was under the curse—and that is tuberculosis. But, then in Galatians 3:13, the Bible said that Christ has redeemed us from the curse of the law.

"So, as much as possible during your waking hours each day, you start saying, 'According to Deuteronomy 28:22, tuberculosis is a curse of the law. But according to Galatians 3:13, Christ has redeemed me from the curse of the law. Therefore, I am redeemed from tuberculosis.'"

And so this woman did. Dr. Yeomans visited her one day and asked her if she had been doing what she'd told her to do. "Yes," she said, "I don't think I slept but ten minutes or so last night. I just quoted the Word. But I don't think it's doing me any good." Dr. Yeomans said, "Well you never mind how you feel about it. You just keep doing it."

So the woman did it that day and the next day. Then, on the third day, Dr. Yeomans was downstairs in the kitchen preparing for the noon meal when she heard a ruckus upstairs. It sounded like somebody was dancing and shouting.

All of a sudden, this woman that had been sick with tuberculosis came running down the stairs with the joy of the Lord in her voice and the gleam of God in her eyes. She reached out and almost embraced Dr. Yeomans and said, "Dr. Yeomans, did you know that I've been redeemed from tuberculosis and that I am healed?!" Dr. Yeomans said, "Yes, I've been trying to tell you that, and I agree with you." That woman rose up from her death bed healed by the power of God!

Now, with this in mind lets look at Galatians 3.

GALATIANS 3:9-14

9 So then they which be of faith are blessed with faithful Abraham.

10 For as many as are of the works of the law are under the curse: for it is written, Cursed is every one that continueth not in all things which are written in the book of the law to do them.

11 But that no man is justified by the law in the sight of God, it is evident: for, The just shall live by faith.

12 And the law is not of faith: but, The man that doeth them shall live in them.

13 Christ hath redeemed us from the curse of the law, being made a curse for us: for it is written, Cursed is every one that hangeth on a tree:

14 That the blessing of Abraham might come on the Gentiles through Jesus Christ; that we might receive the promise of the Spirit through faith.

Now, verses 13 and 14 of Galatians 3 are really the heart of the plan of redemption. This is what Jesus did and why He did it. Notice it says, "Jesus came and has (past tense) redeemed us from the curse of the law." Why? So that the blessing of Abraham might come on us through faith in Jesus Christ.

WHAT IS THE CURSE OF THE LAW?

Somebody says, "What does it mean to be redeemed from the curse of the law? What is the curse of the law?" If we are redeemed from the curse of the law, we had better find out what it is.

Verses 1 through 14 of Deuteronomy 28 list out the blessings. There were financial blessings and there were physical blessings. Health and healing are a part of the blessing and sickness and disease are a part of the curse. If we've been redeemed from the curse, then we've been redeemed from sickness and disease. How? By the blood of Jesus. Where? On the cross of Calvary.

When you get a hold of Galatians 3:13 and Deuteronomy 28, that infirmity, sickness or bondage that's coming at your body or at your mind has no right to stay and to reign in your life.

DEUTERONOMY 28:15-28

15 But it shall come to pass, if thou wilt not hearken unto the voice of the LORD thy God, to observe to do all his commandments and his statutes which I command thee this day; that all these curses shall come upon thee, and overtake thee:

16 Cursed shalt thou be in the city, and cursed shalt thou be in the field.

17 Cursed shall be thy basket and thy store.

18 Cursed shall be the fruit of thy body, and the fruit of thy land, the increase of thy kine, and the flocks of thy sheep.

19 Cursed shalt thou be when thou comest in, and cursed shalt thou be when thou goest out.

20 The LORD shall send upon thee cursing, vexation, and rebuke, in all that thou settest thine hand unto for to do, until thou be destroyed, and until thou perish quickly; because of the wickedness of thy doings, whereby thou hast forsaken me.

21 The LORD shall make the pestilence cleave unto thee, until he have consumed thee from off the land, whither thou goest to possess it.

22 The LORD shall smite thee with a consumption, and with a fever, and with an inflammation, and with an extreme burning, and with the sword, and with blasting, and with mildew; and they shall pursue thee until thou perish.

23 And thy heaven that is over thy head shall be brass, and the earth that is under thee shall be iron.
24 The LORD shall make the rain of thy land powder and dust: from heaven shall it come down upon thee, until thou be destroyed.
25 The LORD shall cause thee to be smitten before thine enemies: thou shalt go out one way against them, and flee seven ways before them: and shalt be removed into all the kingdoms of the earth.
26 And thy carcass shall be meat unto all fowls of the air, and unto the beasts of the earth, and no man shall fray them away.
27 The LORD will smite thee with the botch of Egypt, and with the emerods, and with the scab, and with the itch, whereof thou canst not be healed.
28 The LORD shall smite thee with madness, and blindness, and astonishment of heart:

Now go on down to verse 59.

DEUTERONOMY 28:59-61
59 Then the LORD will make thy plagues wonderful, and the plagues of thy seed, even great plagues, and of long continuance, and sore sicknesses, and of long continuance.
60 Moreover he will bring upon thee all the diseases of Egypt, which thou wast afraid of; and they shall cleave unto thee.
61 Also every sickness, and every plague, which is not written in the book of this law, them will the LORD bring upon thee, until thou be destroyed.

Now remember that Galatians 3:13 says, *"Christ hath redeemed us from the curse of the law..."* When you think about being redeemed—and these are just the ones that pertain to healing—you ought to be shouting! "Glory to God! I've been redeemed from all this!"

I've finally found something in the Bible that doesn't belong to me! Somebody says, "What is it?" It's the curses! They don't belong to me because Christ has redeemed me from them. I am redeemed!

Now, you've got to stand your ground. You've got to receive it by faith and walk it out. It doesn't mean that you don't get symptoms and that you don't get attacked or that you don't feel bad sometimes. The devil will try to bring these curses because he wants to take up residence and he wants to take over.

But you can stand on the Word and say, "You foul devil, back off! You can't have me or my family." He's got to go because you have been redeemed from the curse of the law by the precious blood of Jesus.

A WORD FROM THE LORD

Rise up in faith and proclaim your liberty.
The hour has come for you to be free.
The hour has come for you to walk in liberty.
So rise up in faith, and begin to say,
"I am redeemed, and I am redeemed this day."
And when you do, the anointing will begin to flow
To bring you through, and take you on into
The victory that I promised you.
So, rise up and begin to say, "It's mine.
I have it now. It's mine in this hour.
It's mine by His power!"
And I will perform it in your life, by my Spirit
Saith the Lord.

God really quickened that to my heart. I encourage you to get a hold of this great truth: **We are redeemed from the curse of the law.**

Just do what that little woman did that Dr. Yeomans wrote about. Begin to say, "According to Deuteronomy 28:61, this sickness is under the curse of the law. But according to Galatians 3:13, Christ has redeemed me from the curse of the law. So, therefore, I am redeemed from this sickness," (go ahead and name the sickness, whatever it may be).

When you start acknowledging that, and believing and receiving that, God will perform it for you.

NONE BELONG TO ME

I wrote the following psalm one time and it has really blessed me so much. I know it will bless you.

Sixty-three verses of curses, and none belong to me!
For Jesus took the curse when He died on Calvary.
I am redeemed from the curse of the law.
Thank God I am free!
So there's sixty-three verses of curses,
and none belong to me!

They don't belong to me and they don't belong to you, my friend. They may try to attach themselves to you and the devil may try to persuade you that they do belong to you. But God wants you well. So, rise up and claim what Jesus paid for with His precious blood and begin to say, "By faith, according to God's Word, I am redeemed!" And you know what will happen? The Redeemer, Himself, will watch over that word to make it good. Almighty God will perform it for you.

You are blessed—not cursed. You are the blessed of the Lord.

EPHESIANS 1:3
3 Blessed be the God and Father of our Lord Jesus Christ, who hath blessed us with all spiritual blessings in heavenly places in Christ:

One translation of this verse reads, "…who has blessed us with every blessing that heaven itself enjoys..." I have come to find out that Jesus came to bring a little bit of heaven down here. We don't have to wait until "we all get to heaven" to be healed or to be blessed. Our victory is now. Our redemption is now. God's favor is now.

Take His Word and His name, exercise your faith, claim your healing now, and put that old devil on the run!

LESSON 18:

LAY HOLD OF YOUR HEALING

ACTS 10:38
38 **How God anointed Jesus of Nazareth with the Holy Ghost and with power: who went about doing good, and healing all that were oppressed of the devil; for God was with him.**

Jesus went about doing good, and part of the good that He went about doing was healing all that were oppressed of the devil. Sickness does not come from heaven since there is no sickness there for it to come from.

In this verse, sickness is defined as one of the works of the devil. All oppression is from the enemy. But Jesus went about destroying those works, healing people, and setting them free because God was with Him.

If Jesus ever provided healing, then it is still His will to heal today. As a matter of fact, He took it a step further and provided healing in the plan of redemption in the new covenant for us. All we have to do is lay hold of that rich promise, hold fast to our testimony of faith, and God's Word will come to pass in our lives.

ACCORDING TO YOUR FAITH

In many cases in the Bible where Jesus healed, it was not just a demonstration of His power alone, but it was a combination of the power that He was anointed with and the faith of the person receiving the power.

MATTHEW 9:27-30
27 **And when Jesus departed thence, two blind men followed him, crying, and saying, Thou son of David, have mercy on us.**
28 **And when he was come into the house, the blind men came to him: and Jesus saith unto them, Believe ye that I am able to do this? They said unto him, Yea, Lord.**

29 Then touched he their eyes, saying, According to your faith be it unto you.
30 And their eyes were opened; and Jesus straitly charged them, saying, See that no man know it.

Notice that verse 29 says that it was "according to their faith" that they reached out and tapped into the ability of a willing God. God is all-powerful, and so His ability is all ability. His willingness is all willingness. These men took their faith and they tapped into the ability of a willing God.

You can do the same thing today, right where you are. You can reach out in faith and say, "I believe that God is able and willing to heal me." Then by faith, reach out with your heart, and receive it and begin to thank Him and praise Him for it. Begin to confess it forth out of your mouth as an acknowledgment of your faith and let God perform that miracle. It is according to your faith!

ACCORDING TO THE WORD

LUKE 1:34,35
34 Then said Mary unto the angel, How shall this be, seeing I know not a man?
35 And the angel answered and said unto her, The Holy Ghost shall come upon thee, and the power of the Highest shall overshadow thee: therefore also that holy thing which shall be born of thee shall be called the Son of God.

Now verses 37 and 38:

LUKE 1:37,38
37 For with God nothing shall be impossible.
38 And Mary said, Behold the handmaid of the Lord; be it unto me according to thy word. And the angel departed from her.

Verse 37 says, "For with God nothing shall be impossible." Your situation is not an impossible situation. I can't think of any impossible situation with God as long as we dare to believe, hold fast to His promise, and trust in His Word.

Notice verse 38, *"...be it unto me according to thy word..."* Our faith must be according to the Word because we receive from God according to our faith. If our faith is not in accordance with the Word of God, then we're going to miss out on some of God's wonderful blessings.

The Bible is filled with treasure, and in that treasure chest is healing. There is scripture after scripture of healing for our bodies. You ought to reach out in faith and get a hold of that treasure of healing and health and say, "Be it done unto me according to the Word. My faith is according to the Word." It will be according to your faith that you tap into the ability of a willing God.

Now look at verse 45.

LUKE 1:45
45 And blessed is she that believed: for there shall be a performance of those things which were told her from the Lord.

Mary's part was to believe according to the Word. That's faith and that's your part. Believe according to the Word—not according to what you feel, not according to what the doctors say, not according to what something else says—but according to the Word. Then God is the one that brings the performance of it.

It may not come overnight, but I want you to know one thing for sure: **God will perform His Word for those who believe it.**

ACCORDING AS IT IS WRITTEN

2 CORINTHIANS 4:13
13 We having the same spirit of faith, according as it is written, I believed, and therefore have I spoken; we also believe, and therefore speak;

This scripture says that faith has a spirit about it, or an attitude about it. And that spirit or attitude is that "I am to speak what I believe, and what I believe ought to be based upon what has been written or spoken by God." So Paul says, "According as it is written, I believe."

Don't speak according to how you feel or according to how it looks or sounds, but according to "as it is written." Now, if I believe it, what else is going to happen? I'm going to say it, because he said, "We believe, therefore we speak."

You've got to speak your faith. It's a principle in the Word of God. With the heart man believes, and with the mouth confession is made unto salvation, (Romans 10:10). When we release our faith, we release it with our confession. Base your confession on the Word and get it in your heart. Speak it out of your mouth, and God will perform it for you.

Somebody says, "Well, I can't confess that I'm healed when I'm sick." Well, how come you confessed Jesus to be your Lord when you were a sinner? You see, God calls those things that be not as though they were. When you come to God and accept Jesus as your Lord, you are confessing His Lordship before you are born again. It is that act of faith of receiving Him, acknowledging Him, confessing Him, that causes the miracle of the new birth to come to pass. So, our act of faith is believing His Word, and speaking forth His Word concerning healing that causes that miracle to manifest.

Jesus said, "Do you believe that I am able?" Do you believe He's able? Do you believe He's willing? Then according to your faith, be it unto you. Get a hold of God's promise. What is your faith according to? It is according to the Word. And when you believe the Word, then God performs it, and part of believing it is to speak it. You can't believe it without speaking it because he said, "We believe, therefore we speak."

PUT YOUR FAITH IN GOD'S PROMISE

Now let's go to Mark 5 again, and see these principles put in action in a healing situation.

MARK 5:25-30

25 And a certain woman, which had an issue of blood twelve years,

26 And had suffered many things of many physicians, and had spent all that she had, and was nothing bettered, but rather grew worse,

27 When she had heard of Jesus, came in the press behind, and touched his garment.

28 For she said, If I may touch but his clothes, I shall be whole.

29 And straightway the fountain of her blood was dried up; and she felt in her body that she was healed of that plague.

30 And Jesus, immediately knowing in himself that virtue had gone out of him, turned him about in the press, and said, Who touched my clothes?

In verse 28, it says this woman believed that there was healing power available for her. So she began to say what she believed. What did she believe? What she said. What did she say? What she believed. What was that? "If I may touch Him, I shall be whole. This Jesus is a healer. He will heal me, and if I can just touch Him, I shall be whole."

Isn't that according to her faith? Isn't that according to God's Word? Isn't that according to God's promise? She said what she believed, and what happened? There was a performance: *"And straightway the fountain of her blood was dried up; and she felt in her body that she was healed of that plague,"* (verse 29).

Notice the feeling did not come before the faith. The faith came before the feeling. Many folks are waiting to feel healed before they will say they're healed. It doesn't take any faith to wait until you feel better to acknowledge God's promise. Because faith is the evidence of things not seen or felt.

Faith is always based on God's Word. Faith precedes the feeling. She put her faith in the promise of God, which is Jesus, then she said what she believed, and acted on it. She did exactly what she said. She got a performance—the plague that tormented her life was wiped out by the power of God. Immediately, she felt she was healed.

Now the woman came fearing and trembling and told them all the truth, and in verse 34, this is what Jesus said.

MARK 5:34
34 And he said unto her, Daughter, thy faith hath made thee whole; go in peace, and be whole of thy plague.

There is nobody on the face of the earth that can keep you from getting healed. Nobody can stop you from receiving your healing. Nobody! You know why? Because it has to do with you, your faith, and God and His promise. God has already made His mind up about healing. Now I don't know why some things take longer than others—I'm not an expert on that, but I know the promise is true.

Jesus said, *"Daughter, thy faith hath made thee whole; go in peace, and be whole of thy plague."* God wants to produce peace in your life today. That peace comes from His great provision, and one of His provisions is healing for our bodies.

I'm not going to let the devil rob me. I'm not going to back off and say, "Well, healing must not be for me today," –not when Jesus paid the price that I might be free! What am I going to do? I'm going to say what I believe and believe what I say. I'm going to let Jesus perform His Word for me and healing will be the result!

Now, you rise up and tell that devil to take his filthy hands off of your life and off of your body. You claim your deliverance in Jesus' name. I think sometimes we just don't get mad enough at the devil. We just need to put our spiritual foot down and tell him where to get off.

PRESS THROUGH THE CROWD

There are times perhaps, when we're just not determined enough to move on in. This little woman had to press through the crowd. And you may have to press through the crowd of unbelief, fear, false doctrine, doubt, and skepticism. But you press in. Say, "I believe healing is for me. I am not under that curse. Jesus has set me free." You press on through that crowd and say, "I claim what Jesus paid for."

Don't be discouraged if you don't see results immediately. It takes time for your faith to develop. So get in God's Word and acknowledge His greatness, His goodness, His willingness, and His ability. Claim that promise as yours. Then begin to say what you believe. There shall be a performance of that that has been told you!

NOTES

LESSON 19:

WILT THOU BE MADE WHOLE?

JOHN 5:1-16

1 After this there was a feast of the Jews; and Jesus went up to Jerusalem.

2 Now there is at Jerusalem by the sheep market a pool, which is called in the Hebrew tongue Bethesda, having five porches.

3 In these lay a great multitude of impotent folk, of blind, halt, withered, waiting for the moving of the water.

4 For an angel went down at a certain season into the pool, and troubled the water: whosoever then first after the troubling of the water stepped in was made whole of whatsoever disease he had.

5 And a certain man was there, which had an infirmity thirty and eight years.

6 When Jesus saw him lie, and knew that he had been now a long time in that case, he saith unto him, Wilt thou be made whole?

7 The impotent man answered him, Sir, I have no man, when the water is troubled, to put me into the pool: but while I am coming, another steppeth down before me.

8 Jesus saith unto him, Rise, take up thy bed, and walk.

9 And immediately the man was made whole, and took up his bed, and walked: and on the same day was the sabbath.

10 The Jews therefore said unto him that was cured, It is the sabbath day: it is not lawful for thee to carry thy bed.

11 He answered them, He that made me whole, the same said unto me, Take up thy bed, and walk.

12 Then asked they him, What man is that which said unto thee, Take up thy bed, and walk?

13 And he that was healed wist not who it was: for Jesus had conveyed himself away, a multitude being in that place.

14 Afterward Jesus findeth him in the temple, and said unto him, Behold, thou art made whole: sin no more, lest a worse thing come unto thee.

15 The man departed, and told the Jews that it was Jesus, which had made him whole.

16 And therefore did the Jews persecute Jesus, and sought to slay him, because he had done these things on the sabbath day.

There was a pool called Bethesda, and it had five porches. In these porches were the sick, halt, withered, and maimed people who waited there for God to send an angel down to trouble the water. Whoever was the first in the pool got healed.

This man had been there, or had at least had been in this condition for 38 years. Jesus came up to him and said, "Will you be made whole?" That's a good question. Will you be made whole today? Will you be healed today of whatever disease of infirmity that you have? Most folks want to know, "Will God heal me?" That's not the question here. It's never been the question. God is willing! God is always ready! The question is, Will you be made whole? God is always willing to save the sinner and God is always willing to heal the sick. Just rise up and believe it.

Jesus said to the man, "Will you be made whole?" The man said, "Well, you know, I don't have anybody to help me. When the water gets troubled, I start moving down there, but somebody jumps in front of me and gets in the water. They get healed, and I'm left sick." Have you ever heard that? "It's always somebody else that gets healed or somebody else that gets blessed. It never comes to me."

Well, I'm telling you that it's coming to you today because of the death, burial, and resurrection of Jesus. We don't have to wait any longer. We don't have to wait for the troubling of the pool of Bethesda. You don't have to go to Jerusalem to be healed. You don't have to go to some great crusade to be healed. You can be healed right where you are. Do you know why? Because Jesus said to him, *"Rise, take up thy bed, and walk."*

THE POOL IS STIRRING

Jesus is saying, "I am the pool. I am the pool of Bethesda to you. I am the healing one. I have the healing power. The waters are stirring. You just rise up, take your bed and walk."

He is the healing Savior. He is the Lamb of God that takes away our sins and sicknesses. I want you to know that the pool has been stirred for two thousand years. Many folks have stepped in and got healed. Many folks are still waiting by the pool side. Many folks don't know that the pool is stirring. It's been stirring ever since Jesus went to Calvary, descended into hell, and rose from the dead victorious. The pool is stirring today. You just jump in!

God doesn't want to miss anybody. God doesn't want anybody to miss Him. But there is a move going on. There is healing flowing to you. God wants you to get in and be healed. You say, "How do I do it?" By faith! Rise up by faith and claim your healing in Jesus' name. Receive your healing. Receive your deliverance. Believe you are well and start acting like it.

It was on the Sabbath day that Jesus healed this man and the Jews said to him who was cured, *"...It is the sabbath day: it is not lawful for thee to carry thy bed,"* (verse 10). This man had this infirmity for thirty-eight years, and finally gets healed, and all they could think about was their religious ideas. They didn't care at all about him being healed. Do you remember the statement Jesus made in Mark 2:27? He said that man was not made for the Sabbath, but the Sabbath was made for man.

God is always concerned about you. He's not concerned about the religious ideas that some folks try to put on you. These religious folks were mad at this guy because he had gotten healed. When they rebuked him he said, "Hey, all I know is that this man has healed me, and I am whole. He told me to take up my bed and walk, and I'm just doing what he said. And see, I'm free!" He had received a miracle.

LUKE 13:10-16

10 And he was teaching in one of the synagogues on the sabbath.

11 And, behold, there was a woman which had a spirit of infirmity eighteen years, and was bowed together, and could in no wise lift up herself.

12 And when Jesus saw her, he called her to him, and said unto her, Woman, thou art loosed from thine infirmity.

13 And he laid his hands on her: and immediately she was made straight, and glorified God.

14 And the ruler of the synagogue answered with indignation, because that Jesus had healed on the sabbath day, and said unto the people, There are six days in which men ought to work: in them therefore come and be healed, and not on the sabbath day.
15 The Lord then answered him, and said, Thou hypocrite, doth not each one of you on the sabbath loose his ox or his ass from the stall, and lead him away to watering?
16 And ought not this woman, being a daughter of Abraham, whom Satan hath bound, lo, these eighteen years, be loosed from this bond on the sabbath day?

Verse 11 tells us that there was a spirit that was causing this infirmity. You must understand that some diseases have spirits that cause them. This here, was a spirit of infirmity that was actually attached to this woman and bowing her over. Now, it doesn't say there was a spirit on this other man in John 5, that was keeping him bound thirty-eight years. But, nevertheless, it was still the work of the devil.

Sometimes there is a spirit present. Other times, there's just the work of the enemy involved. But all sickness is an enemy of the Lord because He wants you to be well and strong.

If you've been sick for a long time, don't be condemned. **You can be healed.** You can rise up and receive what's yours because of what Jesus has already done. Now, this woman here had been bowed over for eighteen years and couldn't lift herself up.

In verse 12, Jesus told her, *"Woman, thou art loosed from thine infirmity."* That's quite an announcement! It doesn't say that she looked any different when He said that. But He was announcing her freedom.

Jesus took your infirmity, bore your sickness and disease and you are loosed from your infirmity. Jesus loosed you two thousand years ago!

STORY OF THE GREAT HOUDINI

Years ago, Houdini boasted he could break out of any jail cell, any lock, anywhere. And so some people got together and built a jail that was supposed to be escape-proof. They made a big deal about it, saying that nobody could get out of it.

They invited Houdini to come and to attempt to break out of it. And so, of course, he came. They put him in a straight jacket and locked him in the jail cell, and gave him a time limit to escape. It wasn't long before he got out of that straight jacket. Then he went over and tried to pick the lock of that cell. He worked and worked at it, but couldn't get anywhere.

You could see him begin to sweat—he was getting a little nervous. And he just couldn't unlock it. Then finally, out of sheer exhaustion, as his time was just about to expire, he fell against the jail door and it flung open. It had never been locked.

LOOSED FROM EVERY SICKNESS AND DISEASE

Many of us have been bound by ropes that have never been tied. Ropes that Jesus loosed two thousand years ago. Jesus broke those chains and the door is wide open. It is time for you to walk on through because you have been loosed. You are free!

Now, back in Luke 13, Jesus made the announcement, *"Woman, thou art loosed from thine infirmity."* Then, in verse 13, He laid His hands on her and she received that miracle power of God. She was set free from that spirit of infirmity.

Sometimes, it would be good for us to have a good "laying on of hands" service where you could come and have hands laid on you in faith. But, you know that is not necessary for you to receive your healing. I'm making this announcement: You are loosed by the blood of the Lamb. You are loosed in the name of the Lord. You are loosed by the redemption that is in Christ Jesus and you can rise up and be free from every spirit of infirmity, every sickness, and every disease in the name of Jesus! Take what belongs to you. Receive it and believe it.

The ruler of the synagogue was filled with indignation because Jesus healed somebody in the synagogue on the Sabbath. Where are you supposed to get healed? You ought to be able to get healed in the church. You can get healed in your home, in a hospital bed—anywhere. Surely you ought to be able to get healed in a church. Healing is the children's bread. It belongs to you.

Jesus healed on the Sabbath day and the ruler of the synagogue got so mad that he hollered out, "There's six days in which men ought to work, in them come and be healed, and not on the Sabbath day."

Jesus made a bold announcement to this woman. He said, "You are loosed." That announcement has been flashing from an old rugged cross that is bare, and a tomb that is empty, for two thousand years. Healed, healed, healed! It's time for us to believe it and receive it. The ruler of the synagogue had all those eighteen years to get this woman healed, but he never did.

Always remember this, religion robs you of God's best. It always tries to tell you what God can't do, what God might do, what God won't do, and what God used to do. But relationship with a loving Lord Jesus Christ will build up your faith in a redemption that's filled with healing, health, blessing, prosperity, victory, and salvation. That is Jesus' plan.

Jesus turned and said to the ruler, "*...Thou hypocrite, doth not each one of you on the sabbath loose his ox or his ass from the stall, and lead him away to watering? And ought not this woman, being a daughter of Abraham, whom Satan hath bound, lo, these eighteen years, be loosed from this bond on the sabbath day?*" (verses 15,16) Satan is the one bringing the infirmity, disease, or weakness. He is the one behind it.

Jesus showed up and made an announcement. He said, "You are healed. You are loosed." You see, this woman had a covenant with God. She was a daughter of Abraham. You have a covenant today with God. You are a daughter or son of God. You are an heir of God and a joint-heir with Jesus Christ.

GALATIANS 3:29
29 And if ye be Christ's, then are ye Abraham's seed, and heirs according to the promise.

If you belong to Christ, you are Abraham's seed. This woman was a daughter of Abraham, and she had a right to deliverance.

She had a right to healing. She had a right to freedom. And you have a right to deliverance, healing and freedom today because of what Jesus has done.

What would you do today, if you got an announcement in the mail that said you were the winner of some fabulous prize at a local store? You'd jump in the car, and get down there to see what you had won. We all understand announcements and the value of them. How about wedding announcements? You receive a wedding announcement, and you go to that church or hall because you are expecting a wedding.

I'm telling you, Jesus has announced healing to you today. That's what He did all around the country there in Galilee, and all the areas He went into. He announced the freedom of the Lord.

Now what's your part? **Believe it.** God cannot lie. You can depend on Him. You can bank on His promises. I'm announcing your freedom. Now you act upon it. Expect it, and begin to praise God for it. Simply say, "By His stripes, I am healed." He will perform that, if you'll believe the announcement.

NOTES

LESSON 20:
THE GREAT PHYSICIAN

There are doctors, and then, there are good doctors. There are general doctors, and there are specialists. But I want you to know that we've got a doctor whose name is Jesus, and He is the Great Physician. Praise God for doctors—they help keep the physical body alive. But, nevertheless, there is Dr. Jesus who has come to provide healing for us all.

LUKE 4:14-21
14 And Jesus returned in the power of the Spirit into Galilee: and there went out a fame of him through all the region round about.
15 And he taught in their synagogues, being glorified of all.
16 And he came to Nazareth, where he had been brought up: and, as his custom was, he went into the synagogue on the sabbath day, and stood up for to read.
17 And there was delivered unto him the book of the prophet Esaias. And when he had opened the book, he found the place where it was written,
18 The Spirit of the Lord is upon me, because he hath anointed me to preach the gospel to the poor; he hath sent me to heal the brokenhearted, to preach deliverance to the captives, and recovering of sight to the blind, to set at liberty them that are bruised,
19 To preach the acceptable year of the Lord.
20 And he closed the book, and he gave it again to the minister, and sat down. And the eyes of all them that were in the synagogue were fastened on him.
21 And he began to say unto them, This day is this scripture fulfilled in your ears.

This message was a message that Jesus preached many places, if not every place He went. It was the heart of His mission, the heart of His calling, and what God had appointed Him to do. He said that the Lord had anointed Him to preach the gospel—or good news—to the poor.

There is nobody that is isolated from the gospel. This gospel does not just belong to a certain group. It belongs to everybody. It doesn't cost you anything. It's not cheap, but it doesn't cost you.

It cost Him! So the gospel is available to everybody, wherever you are from, whatever your background is, whatever your nationality is. It's available.

The good news to a poor man is that he doesn't have to be poor anymore. God's got a plan for his life. God can turn things around. That's good news.

Then Jesus said, "He sent me to heal the broken hearted." Healing is right there in the middle of His mission. "To preach deliverance, and to set at liberty them that are bruised or broken down by calamity." God mends broken lives. God mends shattered homes. God heals broken hearts. God delivers those that are bound by drugs or alcohol, or anything that is holding them captive. Jesus preached this message, and then He said to them, "This day is this scripture fulfilled in your ears."

JESUS, OUR JUBILEE

Now, one of the primary things that He said here in verse 19, was, "to preach the acceptable year of the Lord." This whole message centers around who Jesus is, and what Jesus came to do. There is no way that we can doubt that He came to save and to set free, to deliver and heal, and to mend and restore. And He is doing that today. He wants to do that for you .

If you are sick in your body, He is your healer. He is the restorer of your wounded life. He said, "I've come to preach the acceptable year of the Lord." Well, that phrase, "the acceptable year of the Lord" means "the year of Jubilee."

The year of Jubilee was every fiftieth year, and in this year, they were to blow the trumpets in the land and announce their freedom. In other words, if they had sold their ancestry property, that property was restored to them. If they had sold themselves into slavery or servanthood, to serve for a certain amount of years, all the slaves and all the servants were released. Everyone's debts were canceled.

Now that was Jubilee in the Old Testament. What do you think God has for us in the New Testament if all of their debts were canceled? There is restoration and provision. We can announce our Jubilee—our freedom from sickness, disease, poverty, calamity, and bondages.

What is our trumpet? Our voice! Our faith! Our confession! Our declaration! What's happening here? We're believing what Jesus came to do, and that was to set the captive free.

LUKE 4:22,23

22 And all bare him witness, and wondered at the gracious words which proceeded out of his mouth. And they said, Is not this Joseph's son?

23 And he said unto them, Ye will surely say unto me this proverb, Physician, heal thyself: whatsoever we have heard done in Capernaum, do also here in thy country.

Jesus called Himself a physician. He's Dr. Jesus. He is your doctor today, and you can have a visit with Him. You're never going to find His office too busy to see you. He is your Great Physician. He has provided healing for your body. Take this message and hold on to it. Say, "Jesus is my doctor. He is my physician. He is my Jubilee." He will turn things around for you.

I remember reading an account of a young girl that had scarlet fever, which had destroyed her eardrums. She could not hear anything at all. No matter how loud it was, she couldn't hear.

Her parents brought her for prayer and the minister prayed for the young girl. They didn't see any immediate results. But they prayed, claiming her healing, and said, "Lord we release this child into your hands. You are the Great Physician." And the minister never saw the child again.

It wasn't long before this minister got a gift in the mail from the mother of the little girl. It was a nice feather pillow, and a testimony that her daughter's hearing had been restored because of the Great Physician.

You are in good hands with Jesus. Commit yourself to Him and believe Him to bring healing and restoration because He is the healer and He is your Great Physician!

Now you would have thought that this city of Nazareth would have been overjoyed at the fact that the Great Physician had shown up, bringing them the good news about healing, deliverance, restoration, and Jubilee. But you know what they did? They got mad about it. They said, "Who does He think He is? This is Joseph's son—we know who He is!"

They did not see Him for what He was in God. They saw Him from just a natural basis. Do you know that many times you can run into problems dealing with your pastor or minister that way? When you fail to see them in the anointing, or the gift or calling that God has given them. You just see the natural sense as a natural man.

Yes, we are men and we are human beings, but there is an anointing of God on us to bring healing and health and restoration and strength. If you'll view it that way, and receive it as from God, then God will work through that gift to bring blessing to your life.

LUKE 4:28-30
28 And all they in the synagogue, when they heard these things, were filled with wrath,
29 And rose up, and thrust him out of the city, and led him unto the brow of the hill whereon their city was built, that they might cast him down headlong.
30 But he passing through the midst of them went his way.

These people missed the visitation of the Great Physician. Jesus is looking for someone that will believe in Him. These folks rejected Him. So He just passed through and went on His way.

He came to another city and taught in their synagogue. They were astonished at His word, and they believed Him. Demons were cast out and people were set free, and great things started happening because they believed. The other folks wouldn't believe, but these did. Jesus is always looking for someone to believe.

MARK 6:1-6
1 And he went out from thence, and came into his own country; and his disciples follow him.
2 And when the sabbath day was come, he began to teach in the synagogue: and many hearing him were astonished,

saying, From whence hath this man these things? and what wisdom is this which is given unto him, that even such mighty works are wrought by his hands?

3 **Is not this the carpenter, the son of Mary, the brother of James, and Joses, and of Juda, and Simon? and are not his sisters here with us? And they were offended at him.**

4 **But Jesus said unto them, A prophet is not without honour, but in his own country, and among his own kin, and in his own house.**

5 **And he could there do no mighty work, save that he laid his hands upon a few sick folk, and healed them.**

6 **And he marvelled because of their unbelief. And he went round about the villages, teaching.**

The Great Physician showed up, but they wouldn't believe Him. As a matter of fact, they said, "We'll not believe." Then notice that it says in verse 5, *"And he could there do no mighty work..."* In other words, their unbelief had stopped Him from working in their midst. **Unbelief will stop Him from working in your midst and in your life. It takes faith to please God.** It takes faith in His Word to release His hand and work in your behalf.

If He said, "By his stripes you were healed," (1 Peter 2:24), then why doubt it? Why not rise up and blow your trumpet in the face of that disease and say, "In Jesus' name I am healed! The Great Physician has come my way and I receive my miracle today." Then He will marvel—not at your unbelief—but at your faith. And He'll work in your body and in your life. Your faith will reach out and tap into the ability of a willing God, and you'll be set free from that infirmity.

The Great Physician is in town. Rise up in faith and take hold of your healing. Stretch your faith into His promises, and receive it. You have got a right to freedom!

NOTES

LESSON 21:

THE FREE FAVORS OF GOD

LUKE 4:14-20

14 And Jesus returned in the power of the Spirit into Galilee: and there went out a fame of him through all the region round about.

15 And he taught in their synagogues, being glorified of all.

16 And he came to Nazareth, where he had been brought up: and, as his custom was, he went into the synagogue on the sabbath day, and stood up for to read.

17 And there was delivered unto him the book of the prophet Esaias. And when he had opened the book, he found the place where it was written,

18 The Spirit of the Lord is upon me, because he hath anointed me to preach the gospel to the poor; he hath sent me to heal the brokenhearted, to preach deliverance to the captives, and recovering of sight to the blind, to set at liberty them that are bruised,

19 To preach the acceptable year of the Lord.

20 And he closed the book, and he gave it again to the minister, and sat down. And the eyes of all them that were in the synagogue were fastened on him.

I want to focus on verse 19. The Amplified Bible says, "To proclaim the accepted and acceptable year of the Lord [the day when salvation and the free favors of God profusely abound]."

Thank God, we are living in that day. That day when the free favors of God profusely abound. That means they are everywhere. Anybody can get them that wants them. There's an abundance of God's grace and free favors for us today. One of those favors and graces that God has provided for us is healing for our bodies.

Thank God that healing is free, just like salvation is free. It has been provided for us by the Lord. Now, it's not cheap. It cost Jesus a very high price. It cost His blood, but nevertheless, it's free to us who believe and receive it. God's free favors are all around us.

There is more healing available than there is sickness to cause you not to be well. Now in the mind of the natural, that would not seem to be true. It seems like there is sickness on every hand. Yet in the mind of God, the healing He provided in Christ is not only greater in quality than the sickness that attacks your body, but it's greater in quantity. There is more of healing power to heal and to set free than there is of sickness and disease to bring you down and destroy you.

It's always a blessing to know that there is more of God than there is of the devil. There is more of His power available than there is of Satan's work to destroy. There is more life available than there is death. There is more healing available than sickness. There are more angels available than demons. So we can say, "Greater is He that's for us than he that's against us!"

EPHESIANS 2:8
8 **For by grace are ye saved through faith; and that not of yourselves: it is the gift of God:**

Jesus said, "I've come to preach the acceptable year of the Lord and to declare that this is the day when His salvation and His graces will profusely abound." Well, Ephesians 2:8 says, *"For by grace are ye saved through faith..."* So if God's free favors are profusely abounding, then God's grace is abounding. And we believe that there is abounding grace to save the sinner.

The same Jesus that provided His grace to abound for the sinner to be saved, has provided for the sick to be healed. The word "saved" there is the Greek word ***sozo.*** It means "to be saved, healed, delivered, preserved, and prospered."

So we could read Ephesians 2:8 this way: "For by grace are you healed through faith," or, "For by grace are you delivered through faith," or "For by grace are you prospered through faith." **Everything that God has done is an demonstration of His grace.** And all of God's graces are received by faith. The grace made the provision and our faith receives it.

Did you know anybody, anywhere today that calls on the name of the Lord can be saved? By the same token, anybody, anywhere today that calls on the name of the Lord can be healed, delivered, preserved, or prospered because the word "saved" means all these things. Our salvation is all inclusive.

Now the rest of verse 8 says, *"and not of yourselves: it is the gift of God."* What is that gift of God that he's talking about here? Well, most folks would say "salvation" is the gift of God—and that is definitely true. But we've just learned that the word "salvation" has all these other meanings. So, we could say, "healing is the gift of God" or "deliverance is the gift of God" or "prosperity is the gift of God."

Somebody would say, "Well, grace is a gift of God." And that certainly would be true. One meaning of grace is "unmerited favor." I heard someone say G-R-A-C-E means: God's Riches At Christ's Expense. Well, grace would certainly be included in the free gift, but did you know that "faith" is also a gift of God?

Who gave you faith to be saved? God did. Salvation is a gift, but so is the faith to receive it. God's grace is a gift. God gives us the grace, the salvation, the healing and the deliverance, and also the faith to receive them.

GOD GIVES US THE FAITH

ROMANS 10:17
17 So then faith cometh by hearing, and hearing by the word of God.

We access the grace of God by faith, and God gives us the faith to access it. It's sort of like having an access key or an access code. You have a key or a code to access a building or a room of some sort.

God said, "Hey, I've got a room called grace and in that room is everything you'll ever need. I've provided it for you because I love you, and because I am a merciful God. There's salvation and the forgiveness of your sins in that room. There's healing, deliverance, preservation, protection, and prosperity in there. That room is My grace and I'll give you everything I've put in there. It's in My Word, and you have access to all of it by faith. As you read My Word, I've even given you an access key: faith.

I give you the faith to get into the door to access my provision. And faith comes by hearing, and hearing by the Word of God."

ROMANS 10:13
13 For whosoever shall call upon the name of the Lord shall be saved.

We believe everybody is a candidate for salvation. It belongs to anybody in the world. This word "whosoever" includes everyone. *"For whosoever shall call upon the name of the Lord shall be saved."*

Again, we need to expound on the word "saved." We could say, "Whosoever shall call on the name of the Lord shall be healed, preserved, delivered, or prospered." The same "whosoever" that applies to salvation, also applies to healing, deliverance, prosperity, etc. Thank God the gospel is all inclusive and it is a marvelous redemption!

ROMANS 10:14,15
14 How then shall they call on him in whom they have not believed? and how shall they believe in him of whom they have not heard? and how shall they hear without a preacher?
15 And how shall they preach, except they be sent? as it is written, How beautiful are the feet of them that preach the gospel of peace, and bring glad tidings of good things!

God said, "If I can get somebody to tell them what My Word says, they can hear it. And if they can hear it, they can believe it. Because faith will come by hearing and if they can believe it, they can ask for it. And if they can ask for it in faith, it belongs to them."

ROMANS 10:16
16 But they have not all obeyed the gospel. For Esaias saith, Lord, who hath believed our report?

Obviously, some will believe and some will not believe. Some will receive and some will not receive. If we will make up our mind to first hear the Word so that faith can come, then God will perform the Word.

Jesus is our Jubilee. He is our deliverer and He has provided salvation, healing, deliverance, preservation, and prosperity for us. And whosoever shall call on the name of the Lord shall be healed. Healing belongs to you, but you've got to hear it before you can believe it. Hear the Word and let it produce faith in you.

Remember this order: First, there's the promise. Second, there's the preaching of the promise. Third, there's the appropriation of the promise. Fourth, then God performs the promise.

NOTES

LESSON 22:
JESUS IS OUR JUBILEE

LUKE 4:14-19
14 And Jesus returned in the power of the Spirit into Galilee: and there went out a fame of him through all the region round about.
15 And he taught in their synagogues, being glorified of all.
16 And he came to Nazareth, where he had been brought up: and, as his custom was, he went into the synagogue on the sabbath day, and stood up for to read.
17 And there was delivered unto him the book of the prophet Esaias. And when he had opened the book, he found the place where it was written,
18 The Spirit of the Lord is upon me, because he hath anointed me to preach the gospel to the poor; he hath sent me to heal the brokenhearted, to preach deliverance to the captives, and recovering of sight to the blind, to set at liberty them that are bruised,
19 To preach the acceptable year of the Lord.

I want to expound more on this phrase in verse 19, "the acceptable year of the Lord." You remember the Amplified says, "To proclaim the accepted and acceptable year of the Lord [the day when salvation and the free favors of God profusely abound]."

God's free favors are abounding for the asking. One of those favors of God is your healing. It is a gift from Him. Healing came in the package deal of salvation. It belongs to us today because of what Jesus has done. The Bible says, *"For by grace are ye saved through faith..."* (Ephesians 2:8). So then, anything that God does for us is because of His grace.

So God's free gifts and His grace belong to us today and that's what Jesus came to preach.

ACTS 10:38
38 How God anointed Jesus of Nazareth with the Holy Ghost and with power: who went about doing good, and healing all that were oppressed of the devil; for God was with him.

Healing became part of the good that Jesus was doing because He was proclaiming the acceptable year of the Lord.

Now, let's go back to the Old Testament to Isaiah 61, because that is where Jesus was reading from that day.

ISAIAH 61:1-3
1 The spirit of the Lord GOD is upon me; because the LORD hath anointed me to preach good tidings unto the meek; he hath sent me to bind up the brokenhearted, to proclaim liberty to the captives, and the opening of the prison to them that are bound;
2 To proclaim the acceptable year of the LORD, and the day of vengeance of our God; to comfort all that mourn;
3 To appoint unto them that mourn in Zion, to give unto them beauty for ashes, the oil of joy for mourning, the garment of praise for the spirit of heaviness; that they might be called trees of righteousness, the planting of the LORD, that he might be glorified.

Jesus came to unlock your prison. Did you know that sickness can be a prison? It can hold you in bondage. But Jesus came to unlock that door and smash the jail cell so that you can go free. In these three scriptures in Isaiah 61 is almost anything that you would ever need. Jesus came to supply your every need!

LEVITICUS 25:1-9
1 And the LORD spake unto Moses in mount Sinai, saying,
2 Speak unto the children of Israel, and say unto them, When ye come into the land which I give you, then shall the land keep a sabbath unto the LORD.
3 Six years thou shalt sow thy field, and six years thou shalt prune thy vineyard, and gather in the fruit thereof;
4 But in the seventh year shall be a sabbath of rest unto the land, a sabbath for the LORD: thou shalt neither sow thy field, nor prune thy vineyard.
5 That which groweth of its own accord of thy harvest thou shalt not reap, neither gather the grapes of thy vine undressed: for it is a year of rest unto the land.
6 And the sabbath of the land shall be meat for you; for thee, and for thy servant, and for thy maid, and for thy hired servant, and for thy stranger that sojourneth with thee,
7 And for thy cattle, and for the beast that are in thy land, shall all the increase thereof be meat.

8 **And thou shalt number seven sabbaths of years unto thee, seven times seven years; and the space of the seven sabbaths of years shall be unto thee forty and nine years.**
9 **Then shalt thou cause the trumpet of the jubilee to sound on the tenth day of the seventh month, in the day of atonement shall ye make the trumpet sound throughout all your land.**

God told the Israelites, "I want you to rest the land every seven years, and then when you have seven of these seven-year periods, it will be forty-nine years. Then in the fiftieth year, I want you to blow a trumpet of freedom, liberty, and celebration. This will be called the Year of Jubilee."

This is what "the acceptable year of the Lord" means. Isaiah has quoted it to us, Luke quoted it to us, and I believe Jesus preached it everywhere He went, because it was the heart of His calling. This is who Jesus is—the Messiah, the Anointed One. He came to preach deliverance and to heal the brokenhearted, to bind up their wounds, and to set the captives free. Jesus came to preach the acceptable year of the Lord. Really, what He was saying is, "The Jubilee has come. I am your Jubilee!"

Verse 9 says, *"...make the trumpet sound throughout all your land."* I tell you, Calvary's hill was a trumpet sound. It was a blast that's been heard for generations to come and it will be heard forever! Our Jubilee has arrived! The Lamb of God was slain, but He arose from the dead to live victorious. He has conquered all His foes. He is our Jubilee.

LEVITICUS 25:10
10 **And ye shall hallow the fiftieth year, and proclaim liberty throughout all the land unto all the inhabitants thereof: it shall be a jubilee unto you; and ye shall return every man unto his possession, and ye shall return every man unto his family.**

Proclaim "liberty" throughout all the land. Do you know what the word "liberty" means? In the purest sense, it means "freedom and emancipation from bondage." Jesus came to proclaim liberty.

We are not waiting for the fiftieth year anymore. We are living in the fiftieth year. We are living in the Jubilee. Jesus is our Jubilee. We are not looking for the freedom. We are not looking for the liberty. It has arrived!

HOW TO APPROPRIATE YOUR HEALING

Now, it's just a matter of believing that promise, receiving it, and then learning how to appropriate it. So, I want to teach you how to appropriate your healing and the liberty that is yours.

Verse 10 again says,

LEVITICUS 25:10
10 And ye shall hallow the fiftieth year, and proclaim liberty throughout all the land unto all the inhabitants thereof: it shall be a jubilee unto you; and ye shall return every man unto his possession, and ye shall return every man unto his family.

Your liberty has come. We are proclaiming your liberty. God said, "In this Jubilee, I'm going to return every man to his property or possessions. Anything that's been mortgaged or taken away is going to be returned. Anyone that has had to leave his family or sell himself in service is going to be free from that bondage. It's going to be a time of rejoicing! The land will rest. You will rest. And I will give you increase."

LEVITICUS 25:14
14 And if thou sell unto thy neighbour, or buyest ought of thy neighbour's hand, ye shall not oppress one another:

He said, "I want you to walk in love with one another." Doesn't that sound like the New Testament? It is the greatest commandment. You cannot receive your healing and be in strife or have unforgiveness or hatred toward anyone because that will short circuit God's healing power. So, if someone has hurt or offended you, you will have to forgive them. You will have to release them and let them go because God has forgiven you. Then, healing can come.

Then He went on to say, "The fifth thing in the Jubilee is that I want you to walk in the reverential respect, fear, and honor of the Lord your God." So, when it comes to Jubilee in the New Testament, Jesus said, "I am your Jubilee. I am going to restore your possessions. Anything the devil has stolen from you, I'm going to give it back. Anything lost in the fall has been restored."

JUBILEE PLUS

We've actually got "Jubilee Plus." Do you know why? Because we've got it better than Adam did. We've got a new covenant and it is better than the old one. The Bible says we've got a better covenant built on better promises (Hebrews 8:6). So, we've got everything that Jubilee is, plus, He said, "I'm going to restore your family. You may have kids or loved ones that have been out in sin, but I'm going to restore them. I'm going to bring peace into your lives. If you'll walk in love, and walk in honor and respect of the Lord, you can be healed in your Jubilee. This is your hour."

If they had Jubilee in the old covenant, we've got "Jubilee Plus!" We've got restoration of all things. Healing belongs to you. Restoration of all things belongs to you in Christ Jesus. So claim it!

Anything the devil has robbed from you has been restored in Christ. Any family member has a right to salvation in Christ. You have a right to peace and increase and blessing. Now God said, "I'll do that for you. I'll give you everything you need and even everything you want, if you'll walk in love and walk in reverential fear of your God."

Rise up in faith and open your mouth as a trumpet. Begin to say, "Jesus is my Jubilee, and I am free!" Resist those symptoms, claim your healing, and God will perform His Word for you.

NOTES

LESSON 23: FAITH IS NOW

LUKE 4:18,19
18 The Spirit of the Lord is upon me, because he hath anointed me to preach the gospel to the poor; he hath sent me to heal the brokenhearted, to preach deliverance to the captives, and recovering of sight to the blind, to set at liberty them that are bruised,
19 To preach the acceptable year of the Lord.

That acceptable year of the Lord runs reference right back to Leviticus 25 to the Year of Jubilee. Jesus is our Jubilee. One of the easiest ways to understand the Jubilee is to understand that the word itself means liberty or freedom from any bondage of any sort.

There was financial freedom. There was circumstantial change. Jesus provided rest, peace, increase and provision. In the New Testament, we have got "Jubilee Plus." In other words, we have something better than they had in the Old Testament because of what Jesus Christ has done.

TODAY IS YOUR DAY

He was talking about Jubilee. He said to open your mouth and proclaim your freedom from sickness and disease. Proclaim your freedom from poverty and lack. Proclaim your freedom from turmoil and confusion. Proclaim your freedom from sin and Satan. Believe that it belongs to you because of what Jesus has done. We've got a trumpet and it's our mouth!

LUKE 4:20,21
20 And he closed the book, and he gave it again to the minister, and sat down. And the eyes of all them that were in the synagogue were fastened on him.
21 And he began to say unto them, This day is this scripture fulfilled in your ears.

"This day" is a very important phrase. "This day" is the day when God could manifest His healing power for you and bring glorious deliverance and freedom and health and provision into your life. After all, doesn't the Bible teach us that faith is now? It is a present tense word. Let's not put it off until tomorrow. Let's not think about the good old days. Let's think about "today."

"This day" is the day when the Jubilee is on the scene and Jesus will manifest His promises in your life if you will dare believe. This is your day to appropriate God's promise. Remember, faith is now and God works in the now.

FAITH IS NOW

Let's look at this faith in the now just for a moment. This is such an important part of the message when it comes to appropriating our healing. Because many times, folks will say, "Well, God is going to heal me some day," or they may say this, "I believe God will heal me if He wants to." Neither of these statements are statements of faith.

We have already proven time and time again that God wants us healed. When we put things off to the future, we miss that little phrase, "this day." We miss that phrase, "now faith is." We must keep it in the present tense. Faith is now and God wants us well today. He wants us to appropriate His promises now.

HEBREWS 11:1
1 Now faith is the substance of things hoped for, the evidence of things not seen.

Did you notice that there are three things that faith is in this scripture? (1) Faith is a substance. (2) Faith is evidence. (3) Faith is now. My faith in God's Word is substance. It is spiritual substance. Now you may not see it here in the natural, but it has spiritual substance. My faith in God's Word is evidence or proof. And my faith in God's Word is now. The promise of God produces faith in us.

ROMANS 10:17
17 So then faith cometh by hearing, and hearing by the word of God.

When you hear the Word, faith comes. If it is faith, it is going to be present tense. It is going to be now. That faith will be material substance of what you are believing for. It will be the evidence of what you need. Sometimes we wait for physical evidence to prove to us that we are what God says we are. But that is not faith. Faith is the evidence that we need. Faith is the substance that God creates it out of. And faith must be in the now.

For instance, if God says "by His stripes you were healed," but your body says you are sick, then faith in that scripture becomes the substance from which God can manifest the healing. That scripture—not your feelings—becomes your evidence.

PSALM 118:17
17 I shall not die, but live, and declare the works of the LORD.

It would do many of us a lot of good just to quote this scripture. The doctor says that there is no hope. Circumstances say that there is no way. But God's Word says, "I shall not die, but live, and declare the works of the Lord!" When God brings the healing power, He wants you to declare it. When you agree with God, then He begins to perform His Word in your life.

PSALM 118:21
21 I will praise thee: for thou hast heard me, and art become my salvation.

Remember what the word "salvation" means? It means "deliverance, help, victory, prosperity, and health." That is in the present tense. God says, "It's a done deal. I am your salvation. I am your healing. I am your deliverer. I am your Jubilee. I am your health. I am your prosperity." And He says, "I want you to praise Me for it."

How many of us today have simply praised God that He is our salvation? Have you praised Him that He is your healer? You may be facing a long term illness or a bleak future, but the same God that said He forgave your sins, has said He is your healer, your help, and your deliverer. Why don't you praise Him for it?

This scripture here becomes the substance and the material that God needs to manifest healing for you. The healing is already a fact in the spirit realm. God will take your faith in his Word and bring that manifestation in. And this scripture right here is the proof you need.

DR. YEOMANS' STORY

Dr. Lillian B. Yeomans told the story about a missionary that began to praise God for her healing from smallpox. As she was praising God in the spirit, she saw a set of scales. On one side of the scale was her praise basket, and on the other side was her problem basket. The problem outweighed her praise. So God said, "When your praise outweighs your problem, you'll receive your healing. It will manifest."

So she kept praising God day after day. Then finally, she saw in the spirit that her praise basket was full and it outweighed the problem, and she got deliverance from smallpox.

You can praise God because He has heard you. You say, "Does God hear me?" The Bible says His ears are open to the cry of the righteous. There is not one sparrow that falls that God doesn't see. There is not one hair on your head that isn't numbered. God does hear your cry. And if He hears you, then you can praise Him because He said in Psalm 118:21, He has become your salvation.

PSALM 118:24
24 This is the day which the LORD hath made; we will rejoice and be glad in it.

Remember Jesus said in Luke 4:21, *"...This day is this scripture fulfilled in your ears."* Then, here in Psalm 118:24, the Psalmist said, *"This is the day which the LORD hath made..."* He is talking about the day in which we are living. Because he talked about the stone that the builder rejected, and about the workings of the Lord in the plan of redemption. Resurrection morning dawned a new day for humanity, and that new day is dawning for you.

God really has only three days that He talks about in the Bible: yesterday, today, and forever. *Yesterday* would represent the old covenant before Christ. It was a type and shadow of what we have now. *Today* is the day in which we live. It began when Jesus rose from the dead and took His blood into the holy of holies. It was dawning of a new day. This day will come to a close when Jesus returns and receives us to Himself.

We are in the day of the Lord. It is not just a 24-hour period that He's talking about here. It has been almost two thousand years. But God's days are not like our days. You are living in the day that the Lord has made, and in this day, God's free favors are abounding everywhere. They are all around you. They are simply for the asking.

He said, "You are surrounded with My blessings. You are surrounded with My favors. They are abounding. Just ask me for them and I'll give them to you." This is the day that the Lord has made. This is the day when salvation and healing are available to you. You can appropriate them by faith.

PSALM 118:25
25 Save now, I beseech thee, O LORD: O LORD, I beseech thee, send now prosperity.

"Save now." Save when? Now! When is salvation available? Now! When is faith? Now. How do we appropriate this healing? By faith. By grace are you healed through faith. God said, "Now faith is." "Send now prosperity." Send when? Now! God is saying "Now is the day."

Now is the time for your healing. Reach out in faith ,believe it and receive it because God has provided it for you. According to Psalm 118:21: *"I will praise thee: for thou hast heard me, and art become my salvation,"* begin to praise Him because healing is provided. Begin to praise Him because now is the day of salvation.

Praise is the voice of our faith. Praise Him because He has heard you. Praise Him because He has healed you. Don't wait to be healed. Acknowledge that you are healed now. Appropriate your faith and praise God for it. He will bring it to pass.

PSALM 118:27-29
27 God is the LORD, which hath showed us light: bind the sacrifice with cords, even unto the horns of the altar.
28 Thou art my God, and I will praise thee: thou art my God, I will exalt thee.
29 O give thanks unto the LORD; for he is good: for his mercy endureth for ever.

The horns represented strength and power. If a fugitive ran in and grabbed a hold of those horns, he was granted asylum, except in the case of premeditated murder. Those horns represented God's power to forgive and to heal.

Get into the "now" with praise. Get into the "now" with faith. God is saying, "Realize that I have provided it for you. My goodness is yours for the asking. My favors are abounding and if you'll praise Me for them, I'll bring them to pass in your life."

It's a done deal. God said, "I have done it." Done what? He's provided your healing. He says to praise Him for it. Isn't it something that God is asking us to praise Him for something that He says in His Word that we can't see or feel in the natural? That's exactly what faith is. It's the evidence of things not seen.

Remember to praise God because He has heard your prayer. He has become your salvation and He will perform His Word.

LESSON 24: APPROPRIATING GOD'S PROMISES

I want to teach you how to appropriate God's promises by faith. I don't want there to be any question in your mind that healing belongs to you through the plan of redemption. We have seen many scriptures that show us that Jesus not only cleansed us from sin, but also healed our diseases.

1 PETER 2:24
24 **Who his own self bare our sins in his own body on the tree, that we, being dead to sins, should live unto righteousness: by whose stripes ye were healed.**

ISAIAH 53:4
4 **Surely he hath borne our griefs, and carried our sorrows: yet we did esteem him stricken, smitten of God, and afflicted.**

Lesser's Bible says, "Surely he has borne our sickness and carried away our diseases." So hopefully, we have settled the issue in your mind that in the plan of redemption, healing belongs to you.

We have to have faith for that and faith in that before we can appropriate it. It is sort of like saying, "I want to put some salve on a sore spot on my leg." Well, you are going to have to have salve before you can apply it. ***Jehovah Rapha*** means "I am the Lord that healeth thee," and so Jesus is our healer. We have to have faith in that before we can apply it.

THE WOMAN WITH AN ISSUE OF BLOOD

MARK 5:25
25 **And a certain woman, which had an issue of blood twelve years,**
26 **And had suffered many things of many physicians, and had spent all that she had, and was nothing bettered, but rather grew worse,**

Sometimes going to the doctor is not easy, and going through those examinations are tough. I am not saying anything against the doctors. Sometimes the process itself is painful. This woman had suffered many things of many physicians and the sad note is that she had gotten no better. She had spent all she had and was no better. Instead, she got worse. This is a powerfully painful picture to me.

What did she do to appropriate God's healing power? That healing power was in Jesus, and still is. It is in the Word today and it is available to you. Verse 27 tells us what she did to appropriate it:

MARK 5:27
27 When she had heard of Jesus, came in the press behind, and touched his garment.

When she *heard* of Jesus. Romans 10:17 says, *"...faith cometh by hearing, and hearing by the word of God."* So she heard of Jesus, somebody told her about the miracle working power that was demonstrated in His life. Somebody told her a testimony of perhaps how they had gotten healed or someone they knew had gotten free or delivered. And her faith had been stirred because she heard what Jesus had done.

Somebody has to tell you that healing is provided. If you don't know that it's provided, how then can you appropriate it? If you don't know if there is any food in the refrigerator, then how can you eat it? You can't. So you have got to have the knowledge of what is provided before you can release your faith in it.

Now the first thing that happened is, *she heard.* You have got to hear the Word about healing. And the more you hear about healing, the more faith will come to you. So that woman had to hear that healing was possible for her. And I'm telling you it's possible for you, if you believe God's Word. She heard about Jesus.

MARK 5:28
28 For she said, If I may touch but his clothes, I shall be whole.

The second thing she did was, *she said what she believed.* Her believing came from what she had heard.

ROMANS 10:13-15
13 For whosoever shall call upon the name of the Lord shall be saved.
14 How then shall they call on him in whom they have not believed? and how shall they believe in him of whom they have not heard? and how shall they hear without a preacher?
15 And how shall they preach, except they be sent? as it is written, How beautiful are the feet of them that preach the gospel of peace, and bring glad tidings of good things!

SOMEBODY HAS TO PROCLAIM IT

Somebody had to proclaim healing to this woman in Mark 5, and then she believed it. She heard it, she believed it, and then she started saying it. That is such an important step in appropriating your faith for God's healing. Find out what God says about it. Believe what God says about it and then say what you believe.

This woman heard it and she said it. She believed it and she said it. So we see from the point there in Mark 5 that we must say what we believe. We must speak our faith. There are all kinds of opportunities to say what you believe, and whether you know it or not, what you are saying now is what you are believing.

Many times when you are dealing with sickness, the symptoms in your body are talking real loud. They are saying things that are contradictory to the Word. They are saying you are sick, that you are dying, and that you will never get better. Those things are talking real loud, but I want you to know what God's Word is saying: "By the stripes of Jesus you are healed," (1 Peter 2:24). "Himself took your infirmity and bore your sickness," (Matthew 8:17). "He hears your prayers and your cry and He has become your healing and your deliverance," (Psalm 118:21). "Surely He bore your griefs and pains, diseases, and sorrows," (Isaiah 53:4).

When we begin to believe what God's Word says and say what God's Word says, then we are appropriating our faith for our healing.

JOHN 1:19-22

19 And this is the record of John, when the Jews sent priests and Levites from Jerusalem to ask him, Who art thou?

20 And he confessed, and denied not; but confessed, I am not the Christ.

21 And they asked him, What then? Art thou Elias? And he saith, I am not. Art thou that prophet? And he answered, No.

22 Then said they unto him, Who art thou? that we may give an answer to them that sent us. What sayest thou of thyself?

"What sayest thou of thyself?" That is a powerful question. It is saying, "What are you saying about yourself? What are you saying about your situation?" Notice what John answered.

JOHN 1:23

23 He said, I am the voice of one crying in the wilderness, Make straight the way of the Lord, as said the prophet Esaias.

John found himself in the scripture and you can find yourself in the Word. You can find your circumstance and situation in the Word and you can get an answer to your problem in the Word.

God said His Word is our counselor. Some folks are running around trying to get counsel from everybody everywhere on every subject. If we would go to the Word of God, we would find godly counsel. Now, I know there is a time to get counsel from your pastor or somebody, but don't forget that God has given us a book of counsel. He has given us a book of answers and solutions.

When they asked John what he said about himself, he said what the Word said. If you are going to have an answer to your problem, you will have to say what the Word says.

Healing is provided for you, so how are you going to appropriate it? You are going to have to hear the Word first, and then say what you believe. John found himself in the Word and you can find yourself in the Word. Begin to say what God says about your situation.

MATTHEW 16:13-18

13 When Jesus came into the coasts of Caesarea Philippi, he asked his disciples, saying, Whom do men say that I the Son of man am?

14 And they said, Some say that thou art John the Baptist: some, Elias; and others, Jeremias, or one of the prophets.

15 He saith unto them, But whom say ye that I am?

16 And Simon Peter answered and said, Thou art the Christ, the Son of the living God.

17 And Jesus answered and said unto him, Blessed art thou, Simon Barjona: for flesh and blood hath not revealed it unto thee, but my Father which is in heaven.

18 And I say also unto thee, That thou art Peter, and upon this rock I will build my church; and the gates of hell shall not prevail against it.

So there is no sickness, disease, infirmity or devil that can prevail against you when you begin to say about yourself what God says about you, and when you begin to say about Jesus what God says about Him. The Bible plainly says that Jesus took your infirmities and bore your diseases.

Be bold and start saying that instead of what everything and everybody else is saying. Thank God for the doctors and their reports, and for whatever help they can give, but if they ever give you a bleak report and there is no hope; when you are going under and you're not getting any better, but worse, you had better hold on to what God says. And that is the thing that will appropriate His provision.

We believe it because we hear it. Begin to say what God says about it. Say, "I am healed. I am righteous. I am rich. I am well because of what Jesus did." Begin to say, "He is my healer, my deliverer, and my God." I want you to begin to agree with God. Find yourself in the Bible. Find your situation and begin to say what God says. That will put you in line for a miracle!

NOTES

LESSON 25: THE LOVE COMMANDMENT

ROMANS 10:8

8 But what saith it? The word is nigh thee, even in thy mouth, and in thy heart: that is, the word of faith, which we preach;

Now Paul said the Word is nigh us or "near" us. I like to say it this way, "God's healing Word is near us today." The Word that God sent to heal me is near me. If the Word brought my healing and the Word is near me, then my healing is close at hand! It all comes through the Word of God.

PSALM 107:20-21

20 He sent his word, and healed them, and delivered them from their destructions.

21 Oh that men would praise the LORD for his goodness, and for his wonderful works to the children of men!

Do you see why healing is a goodness of God? "He sent His Word and healed them… praise Him for His goodness." God's Word became a source of healing. "Healed" in the Hebrew is the word ***rapha,*** which means "to cure, to make whole, to be a physician or a doctor." He sent His Word to doctor us.

Proverbs 4:20-22 says His Word would be medicine to all our flesh. So there is healing in the Word of God. Paul, in writing to the Romans, said, "This word is near you. It's not some far off, far out, far away situation." We can hold up God's Word before Him today and He will bring it to pass.

We know that Jesus is the living Word and the Bible is the written Word. But I have come to find out that God gave us the written Word to reveal to us what the living Word provided. If you can find it in the Bible, then it belongs to you.

He sent His Word and healed them. Jesus was that Word, and we can claim our healing based on the promises in the written Word. The writer of Proverbs said these promises would be like medicine to all our flesh—so take God's medicine.

ENJOY LIFE

He sent His Word and healed them. The Bible reveals to us God's will and God's plan for our life so that we can believe it, receive it and enjoy it. The word "enjoy" has always blessed me so much because God intends for His children to live in health, wealth, and blessings, and to enjoy life.

JOHN 10:10b
I am come that they might have life, and that they might have it more abundantly.

God wants us to enjoy life. So as we hear what He says, then believe it and receive it, we can enjoy it. Health is ours to enjoy. If you are sick, down, or defeated, I want you to know that Jesus has a good word for you today. He has come to lift you up. He has come that you might have life, and that you might enjoy it to the fullest.

DEUTERONOMY 11:8
8 Therefore shall ye keep all the commandments which I command you this day, that ye may be strong, and go in and possess the land, whither ye go to possess it;

God told the Israelites to (1) Be strong; (2) Go in; (3) Possess. All through this chapter, God expresses His desire for them to possess their inheritance. Look at verse 31.

DEUTERONOMY 11:31
31 For ye shall pass over Jordan to go in to possess the land which the LORD your God giveth you, and ye shall possess it, and dwell therein.

What this says to me is, "You shall enjoy your possessions." I like to say, **Be strong, go in, possess, enjoy!** God wants you to be strong today in His promise and be strong in your faith that He has provided healing for you. Be strong and of good courage because of what Jesus has done. Then go by faith and possess your healing.

Call upon the name of Jesus. Tell that old devil to take his hands off you. Claim your victory in Jesus' name. Begin to enjoy your inheritance—enjoying life, enjoying health, enjoying abundance, enjoying God's best. They truly belong to you!

WALK IN LOVE

Deuteronomy 11:8 says, *"Therefore shall ye keep all the commandments which I command you this day, that ye may be strong..."* He implied that our strength was related to us keeping the commandments. Well, the Bible says to be strong in the Lord and in the power of His might. So our strength comes from His Word. Our strength comes from His Spirit.

He said to be sure to keep His commandments so that you may be strong. Did you know that there is nothing that will weaken your faith like refusing to keep the commandment of love? The Bible says in the New Testament that we are to love the Lord our God with all of our heart, soul, mind, and strength; and to love one another as Christ has loved us.

When we refuse to keep that love commandment, we will be weakened. Our faith will be weakened. We will not be strong because there will be a breach. The number one hindrance to answered prayer is failing to walk in love (harboring unforgiveness, bitterness, resentment, and anger). Failing to walk in love will not only weaken our faith and keep our prayers from being answered, but it can literally open the door to devastation, destruction, sickness and disease.

Until you bridge that gap by forgiving that other person and loving them with the love of God, you will not be able to receive your healing. God said if He has loved us so much when we were sinners, is it too much for Him to command us to love one another? You must deal with that hindrance if you are going to walk in divine health.

If you are going to walk in divine health or believe for your healing in this life, you must be very careful concerning the love commandment. Think about the love commandment in this light: it can be a source of healing, health, strength, and deliverance for you.

1 CORINTHIANS 13:1-8

1 Though I speak with the tongues of men and of angels, and have not charity, I am become as sounding brass, or a tinkling cymbal.

2 And though I have the gift of prophecy, and understand all mysteries, and all knowledge; and though I have all faith, so that I could remove mountains, and have not charity, I am nothing.

3 And though I bestow all my goods to feed the poor, and though I give my body to be burned, and have not charity, it profiteth me nothing.

4 Charity suffereth long, and is kind; charity envieth not; charity vaunteth not itself, is not puffed up,

5 Doth not behave itself unseemly, seeketh not her own, is not easily provoked, thinketh no evil;

6 Rejoiceth not in iniquity, but rejoiceth in the truth;

7 Beareth all things, believeth all things, hopeth all things, endureth all things.

8 Charity never faileth: but whether there be prophecies, they shall fail; whether there be tongues, they shall cease; whether there be knowledge, it shall vanish away.

I love the Amplified Bible rendering of this chapter. If you have never read it, you need to get yourself an Amplified Bible and read 1 Corinthians 13. It says that love is ever ready to believe the best of every person. Love never takes account of evil done to it. Love is not keeping score nor keeping record. Love takes no account of the evil done to it. Love pays no attention to a suffered wrong. That's not always a very easy thing to do. As a matter of fact, without the God-kind of love working in you, you can't do it.

If you are born again today, the Bible says that the love of God has been shed abroad in your heart by the Holy Ghost (Romans 5:5). And that love is in there to cause you to walk in divine health and strength, and to be blessed, and to be a blessing. If God put that love in there, then He has given you the ability to forgive those that hurt you and to release those that have trespassed against you, and to treat them as if they had never sinned.

That is what God does to you. He loved you when you were a sinner, a trespasser who had broken the commandment. And now that you have come to Christ, He treats you as if you had never sinned. God's love is wonderful, and that is the same kind of love that is in us today. That kind of love will put us over and cause us to be strong.

A man or woman that walks in the love of God is not a weak person. Because over there in Deuteronomy 11, God said that if you keep His commandments, you would be strong. It seems to me that our strength is directly tied into the commandment of the love of God. When you keep that love you are going to be strong.

God's Word is your promised land. Go into God's Word and possess your inheritance. Possess your healing. You can be strong by keeping God's commandment of love.

So, if someone has hurt or offended you, or done you wrong, then why don't you pray for them? Why don't' you ask God to forgive them? Your first reaction says, "I'm not sure I want them to be forgiven." I tell you the love of God wants them to be forgiven.

RELEASE ALL OFFENSES

We must release all offenses if we are going to have our healing. Now if someone has done you wrong, you release them because it will determine whether you live or whether you die. So give them to God and let Him deal with them.

Don't render evil for evil. Render blessing for curse. Keep His commandment of love and be so strong that you can go in and possess and enjoy. Did you notice that there is an order there? Without proper order it won't work. Keep the commandment so you can be strong. Then you can go in and possess! God has got a great provision for us today, and part of that provision is divine health. Possess your healing!

NOTES

LESSON 26: GOD'S WORD IS A SEED

FAITH SPEAKETH

ROMANS 10:6-10
6 But the righteousness which is of faith speaketh on this wise, Say not in thine heart, Who shall ascend into heaven? (that is, to bring Christ down from above:)
7 Or, Who shall descend into the deep? (that is, to bring up Christ again from the dead.)
8 But what saith it? The word is nigh thee, even in thy mouth, and in thy heart: that is, the word of faith, which we preach;
9 That if thou shalt confess with thy mouth the Lord Jesus, and shalt believe in thine heart that God hath raised him from the dead, thou shalt be saved.
10 For with the heart man believeth unto righteousness; and with the mouth confession is made unto salvation.

The first phrase of verse 6 says, *"But the righteousness which is of faith speaketh..."* Well that scripture says that right standing with God is going to have something to say. So the righteousness which is faith speaketh.

We teach new believers to share their new found faith in the Lord, to speak what they believe, to give a testimony or a witness to the fact that they have faith in Jesus. That is a principle. If we use that principle in the new birth, then we ought to use it in everything God has provided. The righteousness which is of faith speaketh.

Right-standing that comes by faith talks and speaks. I have come to find out that there are two very important things that God wants us to do: (1) He wants us to speak His Word, and (2) He wants us to praise His name. After all, real faith is learning how to praise God for something that it believes but hasn't seen yet.

In other words, you begin to praise God for your healing because He says it is yours. You haven't seen the healing, you haven't felt the healing, but you begin to thank Him for the provision of it. That is faith and so this righteousness which is of faith "speaketh."

God wants us to say something. He wants us to speak His Word. He wants us to praise His name. As a matter of fact, verse 8 says the Word is near us. Jesus, the Word is near us. God's rich promises are near us. Your healing is close to you today because it is in the Word and the Word is near you. It is in your mouth and in your heart.

We have got to realize that God's Word is powerful and wonderful, but **it will only work for us when we get it in our mouth and in our heart.**

If you are not born again, if you have not received Christ, then that's the way you do it. You believe that Jesus died for your sins according to the scripture, that He arose from the dead, and ascended on high. He has provided salvation and forgiveness for you. You come to Him because of what you believe in your heart, and then you say with your mouth, "Jesus, come into my life. I accept you as my Lord and Savior."

When you do that, something happens. You are a brand new creature in Jesus Christ. Everything in the Word of God works the same way. It is received by faith. It is believed with the heart. It is confessed with the mouth.

ROMANS 10:10
10 For with the heart man believeth unto righteousness; and with the mouth confession is made unto salvation.

Now there is a principle in this verse. It is with our heart or spirit that we believe and it is with our mouth that we acknowledge what we believe. You put those two things together and spiritual law goes into motion and God is able to manifest the rich promises in His Word in your life.

This principle involves anything. You believe unto something and you confess unto something. You believe unto righteousness and you confess unto salvation. You believe unto healing and you confess unto healing based on God's promises.

If He said most assuredly you can be saved, I think you could say most assuredly you can be healed if that is what you are believing for. If that is what you have found in the Word and that is what you are trusting in, then it is yours. We believe it, we receive it, and we acknowledge it. We can thank Him for it.

God is the one that performs it and brings it to pass. Whatever you find in the Word that God says, belongs to you.

BE NOT AFRAID

JEREMIAH 1:8
8 **Be not afraid of their faces: for I am with thee to deliver thee, saith the LORD.**

The first thing God said to Jeremiah was, "Be not afraid." Do you know that fear robs you of God's best. The fear of dying, the fear of disease, the fear of failure, the fear of rejection, the fear of this, the fear of that. You don't have to be afraid of disease because Jesus whipped it. Jesus defeated that disease. He conquered it for you. Don't be afraid.

Start saying, "I shall live and not die. I will declare the works of the Lord." God said first thing, "Be not afraid," and secondly, "I am with thee."

Who is with you today? Who is living in you? Who is walking with you? Who is talking with you? Jesus is! He is with you to deliver you. You can say unto the mountain, "Be thou removed!" And you can say to the sickness, "Get out of my body!" You can say to the devil, "Get out of here because God is with me to deliver me!"

Do you know what that word "deliver" means? It means "to snatch away, to defend, to rescue, to recover, to preserve, to take totally away from, or to take out of." God said, "I am with you to rescue you out of the hand of the enemy. I am with you to rid you from that disease and infirmity. I am with you to preserve you in the time of trouble. I am with you to surely take you out of the bondages and chains and all of those things that would hold you back or distract you."

Let your faith be released. Get a hold of God's promises and claim your healing miracle. He is still a healing Jesus.

JEREMIAH 1:9
9 Then the LORD put forth his hand, and touched my mouth. And the LORD said unto me, Behold, I have put my words in thy mouth.

Did you ever notice that the first thing He touched was the mouth? We believe in laying hands on people. Most of the time, we lay hands on people's heads or their shoulders. Laying on of hands is a fundamental doctrine of the Lord Jesus Christ. It is the law of contact and transmission. The contact of hands transmits the healing power of God into your body. Or, it is a point of contact for you to release your faith in the healing power of the Word of God.

He put forth His hand and touched Jeremiah's mouth. If we don't ever allow our mouths to be touched, it doesn't really matter how much our head has been touched, because eventually, our mouth is going to get us back in trouble again.

Let's be sure we let Him touch our lips so that we are speaking the right things. He says the righteousness of faith speaks. To speak right things is to speak His Word. Too many times we are talking the problem. We are talking the fears and talking the doubts instead of talking what God says. **God's Word in your mouth produces miracles!**

JEREMIAH 1:10
10 See, I have this day set thee over the nations and over the kingdoms, to root out, and to pull down, and to destroy, and to throw down, to build, and to plant.

I am convinced that this is exactly what happens when God's Word gets in our mouth. It begins to root out the problem. It begins to pull down strongholds and those things that oppose God's plan and purpose in your life. It begins to destroy the work of the devil and the works of sickness and disease. It begins to throw down principalities and powers and demonic spirits that are waging war against you and God's plan. And then His Word begins to build you up—build you up in faith, build you up in healing and health, build you up in God's plan and purpose.

There is a building that goes on in our lives as we put God's Word in our mouths.

THE WORD IS A SEED

God's Word is like a seed. As you speak it, you are planting seeds for your future. God's Word will work in you today. The Word will work in you for tomorrow. And you can have healing now. You can have health tomorrow. A harvest of healing is coming your way as you put His Word in your mouth and begin to say what He says.

The righteousness of faith speaketh and when you speak what God says about your healing, it begins to root out, pull down, destroy, and throw down, and build and plant. There is a harvest coming your way. Put God's Word in your mouth and receive your miracle!

NOTES

LESSON 27:

CALL ON THE NAME OF THE LORD

It is one thing to praise God when everything is going great, but praise is such a powerful key in our life that we are to praise Him in the midst of the problem. The Psalmist said "I will praise Him now and forever. And that is when my head will be lifted up above my enemies round about me."

ROMANS 8:31,32

31 What shall we then say to these things? If God be for us, who can be against us?

32 He that spared not his own Son, but delivered him up for us all, how shall he not with him also freely give us all things?

God has manifested His love in Christ for us and toward us in such a degree that He can't help Himself but to bless us in every way. Healing is one of His blessings to us.

ROMANS 8:33-36

33 Who shall lay any thing to the charge of God's elect? It is God that justifieth.

34 Who is he that condemneth? It is Christ that died, yea rather, that is risen again, who is even at the right hand of God, who also maketh intercession for us.

35 Who shall separate us from the love of Christ? shall tribulation, or distress, or persecution, or famine, or nakedness, or peril, or sword?

36 As it is written, For thy sake we are killed all the day long; we are accounted as sheep for the slaughter.

Isn't it wonderful to know that Jesus loves you today and He is just ready and willing to put you over and manifest healing in your life. All you have to do is reach out and call upon His name.

YOU ARE A REIGNING KING

ROMANS 8:37
37 Nay, in all these things we are more than conquerors through him that loved us.

Do you know what "more than a conqueror" means? It means you are a reigning king, but you can only reign after you have conquered. But because Jesus has conquered, we are called to reign. He conquered sin so we are to reign over it.

ROMANS 6:14
14 For sin shall not have dominion over you: for ye are not under the law, but under grace.

He conquered sickness. He conquered the devil and we are to reign over sickness and reign over the devil. So, we are more than conquerors. We are reigning kings. The Bible says we are a race of kings and priests unto our God, and we reign in life by one Jesus Christ, (Revelation 5:10, Romans 5:17).

He said when you put His Word in your mouth, it will cause you to reign. That Word in your mouth is like a two-edged sword. And it will cause you to live victoriously in life.

According to Romans 8, nothing can separate us from the love of Christ. And if we can't be separated from it, then the devil can't stop us from having the benefits of it. Part of the benefits of God's great love for us is healing for our bodies.

It would do you good to simply say, "I'm more than a conqueror over sickness. I reign over disease." Many times the sickness or disease is reigning over you. It is dictating your actions. It is dictating your plans and your schedule. And it wants to dictate whether you live or die. God said you reign over it through Jesus Christ.

ROMANS 10:12
12 For there is no difference between the Jew and the Greek: for the same Lord over all is rich unto all that call upon him.

GOD'S BOUNDLESS RESOURCES

Have you called upon Him? Have you made Jesus Lord and Savior? If you haven't called upon Jesus for salvation from sin, then that ought to be the first thing you do. You ought not waste one more moment before asking Jesus to come into your life. It is not church membership that saves you.

Let's look at several translations of Romans 10:12:

(1) *"...For the same Lord, is Lord over all, is rich unto all that call upon Him."*

(2) *"...Because the same Jesus is Lord over all, He gives richly to all who call upon Him."*

(3) *"...The same Lord is Lord over all, rich in blessing to all that call upon Him."*

(4) *"...For they all have the same Lord and He is generous to all that call upon Him."*

(5) *"...For all have the same Lord and He is bountiful to all who invoke Him."*

(6) *"...For all have the same Lord whose boundless resources are available to all who turn to Him in faith."*

God has got boundless resources for you today. He has boundless resources for your family, for your future, for your problems, for sickness, for symptoms, for financial needs, for forgiveness of sins. There are boundless, limitless resources in God!

(7) *"...For the same Lord is over them all because He is infinitely kind to all that call upon Him."*

God wants to be infinitely kind to you. He has shown that infinite kindness already in Christ. Why don't you believe that and reach out and receive some of His infinite kindness today?

(8) *"...The same Lord is Lord over all and bestows His riches upon all who call upon Him today."*

(9) *"...All alike have one Lord, and He has enough to spare for all those who call upon Him."*

God has enough to spare. There is always plenty with God. He said He is rich to all that call upon Him. Specifically He is talking about financial well being in this scripture, as well as salvation for your soul.

But it would apply to anything that is in His boundless resources, His limitless supply or His infinite kindness. And let me tell you, healing for your body is part of His infinite kindness! He has got enough healing to spare for you.

ROMANS 10:13
13 For whosoever shall call upon the name of the Lord shall be saved.

This scripture is a healing scripture. Whosoever shall call on the name of Jesus shall be saved. When you came to Jesus, you called upon His name without any doubt or reservation. And do you know what happened? You received your salvation, your forgiveness of sin, and you became a new creature in Christ. You got off of one road and on to another road.

You got off the road of death and destruction onto the road of love and peace. You can get off the road of sickness and disease and onto the road of health and healing. The same faith that got you saved will get you healed. The same Lord that heard your cry for salvation will hear your cry for healing.

Remember the word "healed" is the Greek word ***sozo,*** meaning "healing, health, preservation, prosperity, and to be made whole." If you call upon the name of the Lord to be saved, you can call upon the name of the Lord to be healed. It is the name above every name.

PHILIPPIANS 2:9,10
9 Wherefore God also hath highly exalted him, and given him a name which is above every name:

10 That at the name of Jesus every knee should bow, of things in heaven, and things in earth, and things under the earth;

I'm telling you that the devil has got to bow his knee. That demon of sickness and disease, infirmity and weakness has to bow it's knee. You can call upon the name of Jesus for healing today!

PROVERBS 18:10

10 The name of the LORD is a strong tower: the righteous runneth into it, and is safe.

When you run into that strong tower, you are set high above the problem. When you speak that name or call upon the name of the Lord, you are running into a high tower of healing. No devil can get in that tower. No sickness can run in there with you. It has to drop off at the door. It has to bow it's knee to the Name.

ACTS 3:1-5

1 Now Peter and John went up together into the temple at the hour of prayer, being the ninth hour.

2 And a certain man lame from his mother's womb was carried, whom they laid daily at the gate of the temple which is called Beautiful, to ask alms of them that entered into the temple;

3 Who seeing Peter and John about to go into the temple asked an alms.

4 And Peter, fastening his eyes upon him with John, said, Look on us.

5 And he gave heed unto them, expecting to receive something of them.

Are you expecting to receive healing? Are you expecting to be better? Are you expecting God to perform His Word for you? Is your "expecter" turned on? I'm telling you, when you run into the name of Jesus, it carries power over every symptom, sickness, disease, and over every devil. And that demon has got to go. That symptom has got to stop.

Whoever shall call upon the name of Jesus shall be healed. Call upon the Name. Just cry out, "Jesus, save me, heal me! I receive Your miracle power in my life." Then start claiming that and start praising Him for it.

ACTS 3:6-9

6 Then Peter said, Silver and gold have I none; but such as I have give I thee: In the name of Jesus Christ of Nazareth rise up and walk.

7 And he took him by the right hand, and lifted him up: and immediately his feet and ankle bones received strength.

8 And he leaping up stood, and walked, and entered with them into the temple, walking, and leaping, and praising God.

9 And all the people saw him walking and praising God:

He was healed and set free by the power of God. And the people thought Peter and John did it by their own power.

ACTS 3:10-13, 16

10 And they knew that it was he which sat for alms at the Beautiful gate of the temple: and they were filled with wonder and amazement at that which had happened unto him.

11 And as the lame man which was healed held Peter and John, all the people ran together unto them in the porch that is called Solomon's, greatly wondering.

12 And when Peter saw it, he answered unto the people, Ye men of Israel, why marvel ye at this? or why look ye so earnestly on us, as though by our own power or holiness we had made this man to walk?

13 The God of Abraham, and of Isaac, and of Jacob, the God of our fathers, hath glorified his Son Jesus; whom ye delivered up, and denied him in the presence of Pilate, when he was determined to let him go.

16 And his name through faith in his name hath made this man strong, whom ye see and know: yea, the faith which is by him hath given him this perfect soundness in the presence of you all.

Peter said that the name of Jesus was a strong tower for this man. When he called upon the Name for this man's healing, Jesus healed him and gave him perfect soundness. That's why I can say, "Whosoever calls on the name of the Lord shall be healed!" Cry out unto the Name of Jesus. Claim your healing because healing is for you!

NOTES

NOTES

NOTES

NOTES

NOTES

NOTES

NOTES

NOTES